Award-Winning

QUILTS

& Their Makers

Vol. III: The Best of American Quilter's Society Shows 1990-1991

Edited by Victoria Faoro

American Quilter's Society
P. O. Box 3290 • Paducah, KY 42002-3290

All award-winning quilt photographs by DSI Studios, Evansville, IN, unless otherwise noted.

Library of Congress Cataloging-in-Publication Data
(Revised for Vol. 3)

Award-winning quilts & their makers.

   Includes indexes.
   Contents: v.1. The best of American Quilter's Society shows,
1985-1987 -- v.2. The best of American Quilter's Society shows,
1988-1989 -- v.3. The best of American Quilter's Society shows,
1990-1991.
   1. Quilts--United States--Awards. 2. Quiltmakers--United States--
Biography. 3. Quilts--Awards.
I. Faoro, Victoria. II. American Quilter's Society. III. Award-winning
quilts and their makers.
NK9112.F36 1991   746.9'7'097309048 91-11758
ISBN 0-89145-809-3: $24.95

Additional copies of this book may be ordered from: American Quilter's Society
P.O. Box 3290, Paducah, KY 42002-3290 @$24.95. Add $1.00 for postage & handling.

Copyright: 1993, American Quilter's Society

Printed by IMAGE GRAPHICS, INC., Paducah, Kentucky

ACKNOWLEDGMENTS

The American Quilter's Society (AQS) thanks the many quiltmakers included for their thoughtful responses to questions, for the portraits they furnished, and for allowing their quilts to be included in this publication.

AQS also thanks members of AQS worldwide, and all of the individuals participating in AQS Shows – those who have entered quilts, volunteered, attended. Without all of these people, the show and this book would not be possible.

AQS also thanks quiltmakers everywhere, for continuing to produce the exciting work that first made us want to become involved – and continues to make our work a great pleasure.

TABLE OF CONTENTS

5   INTRODUCTION

6   1990 SHOW

92   1991 SHOW

178   INDEX / QUILTMAKERS

179   INDEX / QUILTS

INTRODUCTION

In 1984 Meredith and Bill Schroeder began to make into a reality their dream of an organization dedicated to promoting the accomplishments of today's quilt-makers. Their goals were to develop a membership organization, publish a full-color quarterly magazine for members, hold a national quilt show offering meaningful monetary awards for outstanding quilts, and develop a national museum dedicated to honoring today's quiltmakers.

The American Quilter's Society (AQS) was the result of these goals, with its magazine *American Quilter*, its annual Quilt Show and Contest held in Paducah, Kentucky, and the new Museum of the American Quilter's Society, also in Paducah.

Award-Winning Quilts & Their Makers, Vol. I: The Best of American Quilter's Society Shows, 1985-1987 was published in 1991 to document the first three years of this international show, and the outstanding quiltmakers included. *Award-Winning Quilts & Their Makers, Vol. II: The Best of American Quilter's Society Shows, 1988-1989,* published in 1992, continued this documentation and celebration of quilters and quiltmaking.

For this third volume in the series, AQS re-contacted each award winner in the 1990 and 1991 AQS Shows, requesting permission to feature the winning quilt and its maker, and asking for the individual's current thoughts on the quilt, on the award it won, and on the widespread interest in quilting today. The richness of the responses has enabled AQS to produce another very exciting publication.

The American Quilter's Society is proud to once again present this outstanding collection of quilts and quiltmakers – and looks forward to future volumes. A special thanks goes to quiltmakers and quilt lovers around the world who continue to make each AQS show an exciting event.

Quilt Show & Contest

1990

The sixth American Quilter's Society Quilt Show & Contest was held April 26 through 29, 1990, at the Executive Inn Riverfront in Paducah, Kentucky.

Judges for the show were Dixie Haywood, Pensacola, FL; Becky Herdle, Rochester, NY; Jean Ray Laury, Clovis, CA.

Workshops/Lectures/Seminars were sponsored by Pfaff American Sales Corporation; the Welcome Tea by Hancock Fabrics, and the Fashion Show by Hobbs Bonded Fibers and the American Quilter's Society.

Category award sponsors were as follows:

Best of Show, American Quilter's Society
Gingher Award for Workmanship, Gingher, Inc.
First Quilt Award, Great American Quilt Factory
Traditional Pieced, Amateur, Hobbs Bonded Fibers

Traditional Pieced, Professional, Coats & Clark
Innovative Pieced, Amateur, Fairfield Processing Corp.
Innovative Pieced, Professional, Hoffman California Fabrics
Appliqué, Amateur, V.I.P. Fabrics
Appliqué, Professional, Mountain Mist
Other Techniques, Amateur/Professional, EZ International
Theme: Fans, Amateur/Professional, That Patchwork Place, Inc.
Group, Amateur/Professional, Wrights/Swiss-Metrosene, Inc.
Best Wall Quilt, RJR Fashion Fabrics
Wall Quilt, Amateur, Silver Dollar City
Wall Quilt, Professional, Fiskars
Pictorial Wall Quilt, Amateur/Professional, Viking Sewing Machine Co.
Viewer's Choice, Quilt, Come Quilt With Me, Inc.
Viewer's Choice, Wall Quilt, American Quilter's Society

In each category three awards were made: 1st place, $1000; 2nd place, $800;
3rd place, $500. The Gingher Award for Excellence of Workmanship was a $10,000
award; the Best of Show Award, $12,000; the Best Wall Quilt Award, $5,000; and the
First Quilt Award, $500.

The exhibit included over 400 quilts, representing 44 states and Australia, Canada,
New Zealand, Norway, and Switzerland. Viewers attending were asked to select their
favorite quilt, and a Viewer's Choice Award was made after the show.

The fourth quilted fashion contest sponsored by Hobbs Bonded Fibers was held, as
was a non-competitive exhibit of quilted balloons. Once again, the entire city of Paducah celebrated quilters and quiltmaking with special events.

Dawn E. Amos
Rapid City, South Dakota

The Beginnings

Speaking of her background in quiltmaking, Dawn E. Amos says, "I started quilting in 1978, when my oldest son was just a year old." She continues, "I wanted to be able to stay home with my son and still earn some money. My husband's family are Sioux Indian, and they had made and sold star quilts for some time. His family helped me make my

best of show

1990 AQS Show & Contest

first quilt, which was a Broken Star. After that I continued making and selling star quilts for many years."

THE BEGINNINGS is machine pieced and hand appliquéd, using hand-dyed fabrics. This quilt, inspired by the eagle, is a tribute to Dawn's beginning as a quiltmaker. As mentioned above, her first pieced quilt was a

Broken Star, and her first appliqué quilt, which was completed for the Statue of Liberty contest, began with an eagle.

To make this quilt, Dawn started with seven shades of fabric that she had dyed herself, one yard of six shades and one two-yard piece for the background. When the eagle was done and on her wall, she began to build the rest of the quilt. The design grew component by component – that is what Dawn enjoys doing the most. The vision, on the other hand, comes from serious study and it takes much more time to develop.

Dawn actually completed two quilts for the 1990 AQS show. She explains, "I wanted to enter two quilts into competition that year. I completed SILENT CRIES in nine weeks and had only seven more weeks before the slide deadline for entering the competition." Dawn continues, "It was a challenge to keep the fine detail work in THE BEGINNINGS to a minimum, cut down on the quilting, and yet come up with a well balanced quilt."

Asked if she would do anything differently if she were beginning to make this quilt today, Dawn quickly replies, "I would have spent much more *time* on it, if I had had it!"

About the effect of this award on her life, Dawn says, "Winning this award has been like a dream come true. On one hand, I have had a difficult time accepting the fact I have won, because I didn't think the quilt was good enough. But, winning has been a great honor, and has increased the value of my work and also my self-confidence." Thinking again of the surprise, Dawn adds, "I heard it had been named Best of Show Winner on the radio, and sometimes I still find it hard to believe."

"Quilting is addictive. Once you start, you can't stop – there is that part of you that just wants to keep getting better and better."

THE
BEGINNINGS
64" x 84"
1989
Dawn E. Amos

Nancy Ann Sobel
Brooktondale, New York

A Midwinter Night's Dream

Nancy Ann Sobel comments, "This quilt is the winter quilt in my series on the seasons, so I wanted a star pattern since the other three quilts were stars. Crown of Thorns, an old traditional pattern and one of my very favorites, seemed the perfect choice for my needs. My own imagination took over from there, with snowflakes, use of cool colors, and some flowers and leaves for anticipation of spring."

gingher award

for workmanship
1990 AQS Show & Contest

The overall quilt design is original, and Nancy used 100% cotton for both the top and backing, with low loft polyester batting. It includes applique, some piping around the border, machine piecing, and hand quilting, in echo quilting, grid quilting, and other designs.

Nancy says that in making this quilt she learned much about design, and also about the value of goal setting, journal keeping, and the patience that it takes to pursue excellence.

Nancy explains that she is actually making this quilt again for her daughter, Tammy, who was to inherit the first quilt. She adds, "The colors are the same, but fabrics could not be matched exactly. I had to reverse the solid gray and the print, and I designed my own flowers and leaves to make this quilt unique for Tammy. I think I might put a little more white in the border somehow, to complement the white in the center, and add some tiny

embroidery on the outer lavender scallop."

About her background, Nancy says, "I started my first quilt when I was 13 years old, assisted and influenced by my grandmother, but I put it aside in favor of dressmaking and other more exciting things until marriage. Then I made a very simple patchwork quilt using scraps cut into squares.

"Next came a baby quilt, which wasn't quilted until the 'baby' was almost 16 years old. That is when my present quilting activity really began in earnest. I remain an old-fashioned person. I enjoy a simple lifestyle with my family in the country, working with my hands (braided rugs, chair caning, sewing, furniture refinishing, gardening), walking, studying art and designing on my own, and studying the Bible."

Asked about her 1990 AQS award, Nancy says, "For me, winning this particular award was like receiving an unexpected special gift, undeservedly. I still feel very humbled and amazed, remembering all those other wonderful quilts which I felt

"Before it was quilted I liked this quilt the least of those in my seasons series, but it has turned out to be my favorite. Through it, I learned about the beauty of simplicity of design and the enhancement of various quilting designs."

A MIDWINTER
NIGHT'S
DREAM
99" x 99"
©1988
Nancy Ann
Sobel

far surpassed mine in quality, design and workmanship." Nancy adds, "Completing this quilt, or any project, makes me feel somewhat like a winner for the personal satisfaction it gives of finishing something I've started."

Lucy Burtschi Grady
Albuquerque, New Mexico

Kaleidoscope Stars

Lucy Burtschi Grady says of her background, "I grew up in a quilting family. My mother and my aunts quilted for both our family and a church group. I remember my mother trading quilt patterns with women at church and with the women in families who were buying real estate from my father."

first place

1990 AQS Show & Contest Traditional Pieced, Ama

Lucy continues, "Neither my sister, Jane Hodge, nor I ever thought we'd quilt when we got older. But when Mom came to visit us she would often start a quilt, and naturally, we would help. This kept us supplied with quilts. At the time I thought of them more as necessities than beautiful works of art. But of course they were pretty, and some had the sentimental value of this or that piece having come from a child's dress or a friend's blouse.

"I began quilting in earnest after my children were grown and out of the

house. My youngest was away at graduate school in 1976, and a lot of people I knew were making bicentennial quilts. My sister and I each decided to make one. We were surprised at how much we enjoyed it, and it soon became an avocation."

KALEIDOSCOPE STARS, which Lucy believes is her 52nd quilt, grew out of a class taken by her friend Charlotte Beyer. Stars made of striped fabric piqued Lucy's interest. She explains, "I started it from some scraps of a fabric I'd put on the back of a picture quilt. I was going

on a trip, so I took along my usual busy kit. That time I took striped fabric and an Eight Point Star pattern."

The pattern in this hand- and machine-pieced and hand-quilted quilt is a variation on the Nine Patch and Eight Point Star. Lucy comments, "It intrigued me to see that I could, by careful cutting, make many variations with striped fabric. Every star in this quilt looks different, though all are cut from the same material." Lucy has been so fascinated by this project that she has started two more star quilts using different striped fabrics.

Speaking of her award, Lucy says, "Completing any quilt never fails to give me a feeling of satisfaction — or is it relief! To win recognition for work I love is even more satisfying. My family teases me about being a 'famous quilter,' but I have never thought of myself as any kind of celebrity."

Asked why she feels there is such interest in quiltmaking, Lucy replies, "I think the social aspects of quilts and quiltmaking account for the interest. Quilting is great for

"This quilt is a good example of what I enjoy doing – using traditional techniques and patterns while making creative changes unique to me."

KALEIDOSCOPE
STARS
76" x 84"
1990
Lucy Burtschi
Grady

making friends. You share the work, and, while working with bits and pieces of fabric, you share bits and pieces of one another's lives. Quilting could almost be considered a 'team sport.' I greatly enjoy the camaraderie and the exchange of ideas."

Karen Kratz-Miller
Cincinnati, Ohio

Blueprints

Inspired by her love of scrap quilts and the Schoolhouse pattern, Karen Kratz-Miller conceived BLUEPRINTS "while living in a blue stucco bungalow in Oakland, California." She explains that she drafted the house block from a Schoolhouse pattern in *Quilter's Newsletter Magazine* – eliminating the second chimney and reversing the house in some blocks. She

second place

1990 AQS Show & Contest
Traditional Pieced, Ama

adds, "After separating my mostly blue fabrics into piles of light, medium, and dark values, and collecting warm yellow and orange accents, I built the houses block by block on the dining room table. While the pattern pieces are identical in every block, each house has its own personality and landscaping, the time of day changing with varying fabric skies, shadows, and window glows. The finished blocks were then arranged on the floor into neighborhoods, the

houses fenced off with dark blue sashing, and the 'pieceful' town bordered by stripped mountainscapes and Log Cabin corners. Parallel hand quilted lines accent architectural elements and fabric designs."

Asked if she would do anything differently if starting BLUEPRINTS today, Karen replies, "I would design the quilt on the wall before doing any sewing." But she adds, "I'm very pleased with BLUEPRINTS as it is now — there's a lot to be said for the element of chance."

About her background

Karen says, "I began quilting in 1977, working in creative spurts between caring for my young children and holding an outside job. A full-time quiltmaker since 1989, I show my work in shows and exhibitions, and teach and lecture on color and design."

Speaking of the effects of her award, Karen says, "Non-quilting friends took my work more seriously and the cash award helped me purchase a new and much improved sewing machine."

Karen says about quiltmaking: "The functions of a quilt are as varied as the people who make them. As quiltmakers, our styles, approaches, and goals differ, but each of us responds primarily to the visual and tactile quality of fabric. I cannot imagine a painter or potter exclaiming over the newest paint or clay or glaze, and hoarding these materials, sometimes to the exclusion of producing a painting or pot. Have you ever met an artist proud (or guilty) of her stockpile of materials, and proclaiming herself to be a clay collector or paint-aholic?"

"I have always made quilts that interest and excite me, and because my focus is so self-directed and non-beauty oriented, I'm always somewhat surprised when others like and respond to my work."

BLUEPRINTS
70" x 90"
1989
Karen
Kratz-Miller

Beverley Cosby
Mechanicsville, Virginia

Molly's Star

Beverley Cosby says of this quilt's design, "I love Eight Point Star patterns. In fact, I've even done a sampler quilt with eleven different Eight Point Star Patterns. A traditional name for MOLLY'S STAR is Carpenter's Wheel." She adds, "Carpentry and building were my father's profession. When I saw a quilt in *Lady's Circle Patchwork Quilts* done in this pattern, I realized I just had to make it."

third place

1990 AQS Show & Contest Traditional Pieced, Ama

The quilt is constructed in all-cotton fabrics with extra-loft batting, and is hand pieced and hand quilted. Speaking of the quilt's development, Beverley says, "The quilt was originally to have been the green that I did use and muslin, but the two just weren't right together. I had the green three or four years before I finally found the paisley and 'solid' print, which I thought were just right."

Asked if she would do anything differently if making the quilt today, Beverley says, "No, I spent considerable time picking the fabric and quilting designs. I made the quilt many times in my mind before I ever touched a piece of fabric."

Beverley explains about her background: "My grandmother, Molly, for whom this

quilt was named, was a quilter. We used her quilts, not blankets, when I was a child. I loved the colors and feel of them. Although I sewed and did other needlework, I never thought about making quilts until one year at the State Fair I saw a beautiful Dresden Plate scrap quilt, the best of show winner. I realized I'd give almost anything to have it. I couldn't have that one, so I decided to try quilting and make one myself. I began with a kit for an embroidered quilt and progressed from there with the help of various magazines and books."

Asked why there is such interest in quiltmaking today, Beverley replies, "I've often thought about it, but it's a mystery to me. I just know I love to quilt: it's relaxing and stimulating at the same time, and it gives me pleasure and a feeling of accomplishment when a quilt is finished. I can only think that it affects other people the same way."

"I envy people who can go to a shop and pick all the fabrics for quilt at one time – sometimes it takes me several years!"

MOLLY'S STAR
80" x 96"
1989
Beverley Cosby

Margie T. Karavitis
Spokane, Washington

Oh, My Stars

Speaking of her introduction to quiltmaking, Margie T. Karavitis explains, "I decided to make a quilted coverlet when I needed a new bedspread for a high four-poster bed." She adds, "The coverlet was completed in 1972. Now, I can't imagine not having quilts in the making. I've learned that it is best if I have one being pieced or appliquéd so that when I take a quilt off the frame, I have another ready to be quilted."

first place

*1990 AQS Show & Contest
Traditional Pieced, Pro*

Margie explains that the inspiration for OH, MY STARS was an antique quilt pictured in *America's Glorious Quilts*. She discusses the quilt's development from this inspiration, "First, I changed from scrap stars to a more controlled color scheme. Then, when I was ready to sew the blocks together, I felt the quilt was not balanced, so I re-arranged the blocks until a very different quilt emerged." She adds, "Even though someone else's quilt was the inspiration, OH MY STARS turned out to be my quilt."

Margie used an extra-loft batt and lots of background quilting. She comments, "I outline quilted the stars and squares, which makes them appear to be stuffed. I also used trapunto and stipple quilting in selected areas of the quilting pattern."

Asked if she would do anything differently if she were beginning the quilt today, Margie says, "I

wouldn't make dozens of three-inch scrap stars! As the work progressed, I decided that I did not like the scrappy look, so changed to two shades of pink and blue."

In response to a question about the effect of her award, Margie says, "Winning an award for my quilting has given me confidence to try other techniques; however, I find that I still like to make traditional quilts with muslin, pastels, and lots of quilting."

About the popularity of quiltmaking, Margie says, "I'm not sure why the interest in quiltmaking is so great – or why quiltmaking is different. I only know that it is! I've asked several quilters and non-quilters and get a different answer from each one. My daughter has used quiltmaking in her special education class with unexpected and wonderful results. Students who were not at all motivated responded with interest and pride in their work. My granddaughter says she likes making quilts because you can do what you want, and when you are finished, you can wrap up in them."

"I think making quilts gives us a connection to the traditions and values of the past."

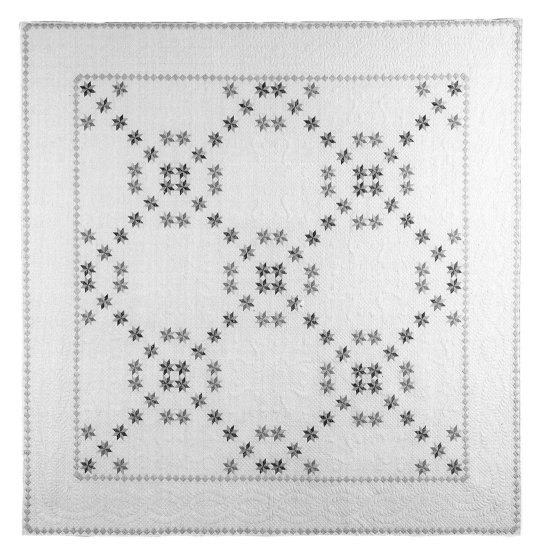

OH, MY STARS
97" x 97"
1989
Margie T.
Karavitis

Julia Overton Needham
Knoxville, Tennessee

Anemones

"Needlework has fascinated me ever since I was able to hold a needle," says Julia Overton Needham, when asked about her quilting background. She continues, "I've covered the gamut of needlework, with the exception of tatting, which turned out to be my nemesis. Remembering the quilting revival of the 1930's, I turned to quilting in later life." She adds, "The Depression evidently made a very lasting impression on me in childhood. Even today, I still use scraps and only buy the 'fill-in' fabrics needed."

second place

*1990 AQS Show & Contest
Traditional Pieced, Pro*

Speaking of the development of ANEMONES, Julia says, "As with all my quilts, the inspiration for this quilt originated with fabric, one piece of striped fabric bought on a whim." She adds, "The pattern used is the classic Courthouse Steps set for Log Cabin blocks."

This quilt is made of cottons and cotton blends with most fabrics having a black thread woven throughout, and it is machine pieced and hand quilted. "The entire quilt was laid out before piecing," says Julia. "The border was originally meant to be the quilt backing, but I

Photo: Joyce Lennery

discovered that the colors in that fabric were harmonious with the top. Some judges haven't agreed with me. They have given both positive and negative comments on the use of that border fabric, although they have all given ANEMONES a blue ribbon."

Asked if she would do anything differently if making the quilt today, Julia says, "I wouldn't change a thing. I would, though, take more time to improve the quality of my workmanship – I always feel that way about my quilts."

Commenting on her award, Julia says, "I have received much recognition, which is immensely gratifying, for doing something I thoroughly enjoy."

About quilting she says, "Interest in quilts seems to be universal – everybody identifies with them. They want to see them and they are anxious to tell everyone about their own mother's or grandmother's quilts."

I loved making this quilt. Every day I looked forward to cutting the pieces and arranging them."

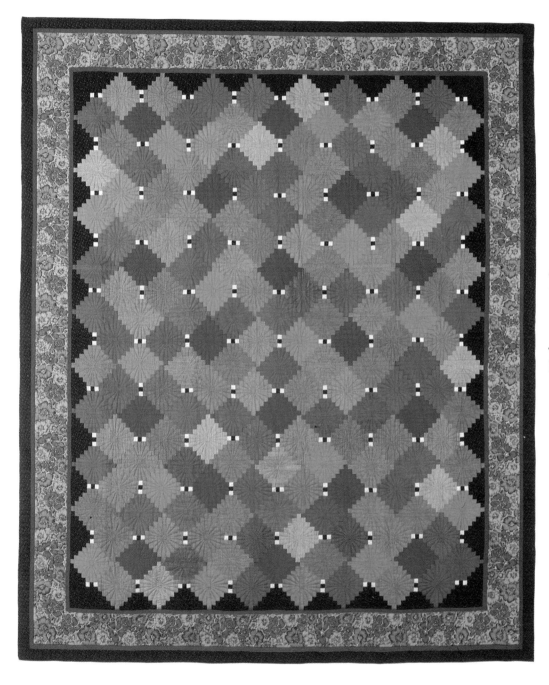

ANEMONES
75" x 90"
1988
Julia Overton
Needham

Judy Spahn
Clifton, Virginia

Flywheels

The design for this quilt is original, but Judy Spahn explains that it is similar to Sand Dollar, a design found in Jinny Beyer's book *Patchwork Portfolio*.

She comments, "I began quilting in the early 1970's, while my children were still small. Quilting provided an opportunity to develop close friendships, to create something useful, and to be creative, even though I had no art training. I began creating my own geometric patterns shortly after Jinny Beyer wrote *Patchwork Patterns*. This volume and my background in math have been major influences on the way I make quilts."

third place

*1990 AQS Show & Contest
Traditional Pieced, Pro*

Judy started teaching at Jinny Beyer's Seminar on Hilton Head Island, SC, in 1981. That exposure and the resulting self-confidence have allowed her to branch out into other areas. She

explains, "I teach and lecture occasionally, and belong to a quilt art group that shows in galleries. I have done commissioned work and also published and marketed patterns. I currently work part time for RJR Fashion Fabrics, assisting in the design and setting up of displays for quilt markets."

Speaking of the development of FLYWHEELS, Judy says, "The quilt uses different fabrics in every block. The fabric choices are not traditional calicoes, but rather an assortment of textures. The first block was made to demonstrate the use of plaids, stripes, and large prints to a quilt class. I continued making these blocks just for the pleasure I derived from seeing the fabrics interact. After making twenty, I decided I should make a quilt."

Judy says the most challenging part of making this hand-pieced and hand-quilted work was "finding a background fabric that would not overpower the blocks."

Of her award, Judy says, "Winning this award was one of the most exciting surprises of my quilting career." She adds, "Rather than have the prize money just disappear, I bought mountain bikes for my husband and myself. He was delighted!"

Judy believes one of the most important reasons quiltmaking is so popular today is that it "is a flexible activity. It can fill the needs of many people at all stages of their lives. It can be soothing or it can be exciting, depending on the type of quilt one chooses to make."

"I quilt for the thrill of discovery. I like to try something new, whether it is a new design, a new fabric, or an attempt to create a new effect."

FLYWHEELS
80" x 92"
1990
Judy Spahn

Becky Brown
Richmond, Virginia

Rhapsody In Threads

"It was my Grandmother, Bhlandena 'Bobe' Hull Barnes, who made quilts a natural part of my life," explains Becky Brown. "At age eight she invited me to join her at the quilting frame. There was never a suggestion that quilting was something one learned; it was simply something one did.

first place

1990 AQS Show & Contest Innovative Pieced, Ama

"So before my first child was born 24 years ago, I completed my first quilt without ever asking anyone how. As the years passed and my interest in quilting and design progressed, I came to realize that this was the avenue of artistic expression that offered a satisfaction I had never known. At last, I had found the way to release the silent voice within me, blend it with basic skills, and like my grandmothers, leave it as my gift to the future."

About this quilt, Becky says, "Inspiration to make RHAPSODY IN THREADS had two components: the death of a dear friend had left me feeling very sad. One morning an upbeat song lifted my spirits. While listening to that song I decided to stop feeling sad and begin being happy again. That night I began a quilt whose purpose was to make me feel good.

"Additional inspiration came from the raveled threads I collect. Washing fabric produces lots of raveled threads which I carefully trim after the fabric has been through the dryer. I had no plan when I impulsively began sewing fabric and thread sculptures together. I

worked intensely, using bright colors, which was a bold break from my trademark blue/mauve/purple combinations of the past."

The quilt is constructed of machine pieced cotton fabrics, and includes thousands of glass beads, which are an important design element, and squiggly shapes appearing on the solid rainbow colored fabrics, which are the sculptures created from raveled threads.

Becky's work has won many awards. She makes several quilts each year, in addition to working full time for a printing company, and she is the founder of the Helping Hands Quilt Project, a nonprofit organization that gives quilts to people (especially children) who are homeless, abused or critically ill.

About her award, Becky says, "Winning a first place AQS award means success in reaching one of my goals. After winning a large cash award, my friends seem to view me with greater respect. Hopefully, that respect will rub off onto other dedicated quilters and we will all be seen in a more serious light."

"The AQS award has given me added confidence to listen to my inner voice and reach deeper within myself to create quilts that are more personally meaningful."

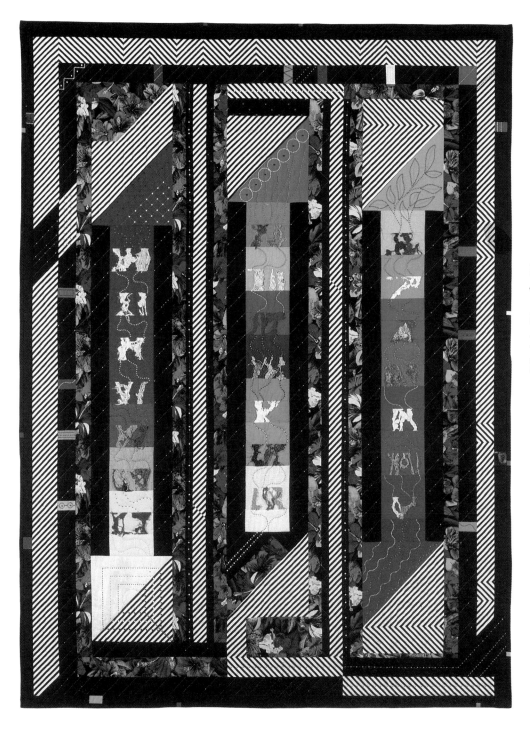

RHAPSODY IN
THREADS
64.5" x 87"
1989
Becky Brown

Betty A. Lenz
Marshall, Missouri

Tokay Bouquet

Betty A. Lenz says that when she began this quilt, she really wanted to change her usual scope of colors. She explains, "I attended a seminar in Nebraska in 1988 and closely studied several of Jinny Beyer's quilts, hoping some of her color sense would affect my fabric selections. I came home with about 30 new fabric colors and started building on those. I chose the County Fair block pattern for its complexity, and because it would allow me to work with many colors."

second place

1990 AQS Show & Contest
Innovative Pieced, Ama

Betty says she did several border treatments for this entirely hand-pieced quilt before she found the one she liked. She elaborates, "As I was considering the idea of adding appliquéd grapes, I asked several quilters their opinions. Most said, 'Don't do it – it doesn't need it' or 'Why risk spoiling a nice quilt?' Even as I listened to these comments, I knew I was going to try it, just to prove it could be effective."

There were reasons why Betty was ready to try something new. She explains, "I had found myself almost bored with quilting. Because of limited fabric availability, I felt my quilts all looked alike; there was no freshness, no spark. It was just more of the same. To keep from getting in a rut, it is very necessary to periodically turn yourself around and go in a new direction. Quilters need to assess their work on a regular basis and make themselves do a few things out of character. They must try new things."

Betty says of her background, "I have been sewing all my life. I can remember my mother having to cut me loose from doll clothes stitched to the hem of my dress when I was a child. I have also been quilting for many years, but really got serious about 12 years ago."

About the award, Betty comments, "This was the first time I had ever entered a quilt in competition, never mind a national show. To win an award the first time was staggering! I will never forget the entire experience. I smiled for weeks afterward."

Asked to comment on quilting in general, Betty says, "Quilts are very precious because of their lasting ability. You are creating something with a possible 100-year life. Most other crafts outwear their welcome in several years. That is not the case with quilts."

"I can't work from a totally planned idea. I have to let a few things just happen! Accidents are sometimes so refreshing."

TOKAY
BOUQUET
83" x 98"
1989
Betty A. Lenz

Joy Baaklini
Austin, Texas

Satin Pinwheels

"SATIN PINWHEELS," explains Joy Baaklini, "was based on a crocheted piece from the 1930's or 1940's found in a box of things from my grandmother. As soon as I saw the crochet work I wanted to translate it into a quilt, to give my own interpretation of color and form to the pattern. Almost immediately I was immersed in my first strip-piecing effort.

third place

*1990 AQS Show & Contest
Innovative Pieced, Ama*

"To draft the pattern, I placed the crochet work on my light table. After tracing the shapes, I enlarged the hexagon unit on triangular graph paper, created the four templates, and rotary cut the shapes. Strip piecing allowed me to vary the values from light to dark in each band of eight 1" strips, so I was able to create the illusion of light and space, giving SATIN PINWHEELS its dimensional quality."

Joy adds, "One should always be open to the unexpected. Not knowing how many hexagons I would make, I didn't figure yardage, preferring instead to use fabric from my collection. Substitutions became necessary. The variations between pink and green on the pastel sides of the dark bands are my 'happy' accidents, which created the shimmering effect."

About her background, Joy says, "Like many, I began quilting with a 'small' project (making patchwork blocks to use as pillows). Penny McMorris' first series on PBS inspired me to turn the blocks into a sampler quilt. In 1986, I began to branch out into the demanding

world of contemporary quilt art. Since SATIN PINWHEELS, I have completed several more difficult quilts and now long to return to the comforting work of a traditional quilt. I want to make more bed quilts while I can still manage the fine hand quilting!"

She continues, "Maintaining a high level of commitment for the long time it takes to complete a quilt is exhausting. I am obsessed with the initial design stages until I am able to zero-in on what the quilt needs. Then satisfying that need takes precedence over most other concerns! As you can imagine, parts of my life are in total disarray from constantly being pushed to the back burner as I solve design problems and construct new works." About the design of this quilt, Joy says, "Next time I would make the quilt a square or rectangle. Large odd-shaped quilts create nightmare hanging problems. Plus, for this quilt I had to miter six corners!"

Of her award, Joy says, "Each award that I win gives me some tangible evidence that my work communicates

"Through quilt shows, workshops, and magazines all quilters can be inspired by the collective energy of the revived quilting movement. Women speak to women directly and indirectly, in their work and in what they have to say about it."

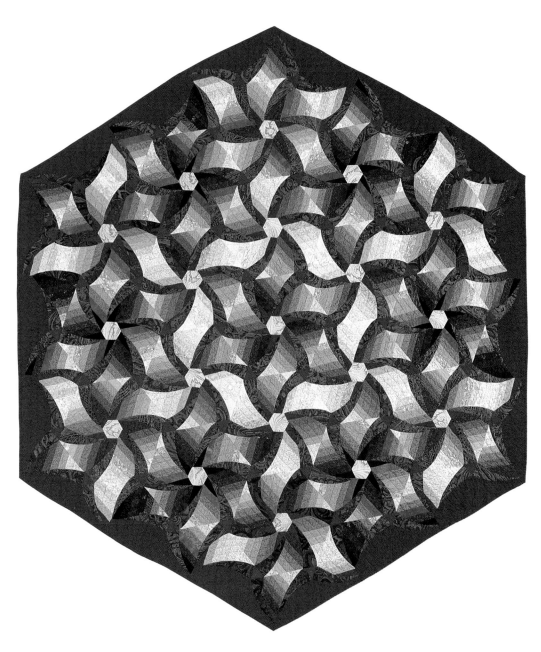

SATIN
PINWHEELS
82" x 82"
1989
Joy Baaklini

with others; feeling stronger in myself and as an artist, I am better able to move on to whatever 'comes next' in my development as a quilter, whether it be an even more challenging contemporary piece or a return to the comforting structure of a traditional bed quilt, with its rhythms of piecing and hand quilting."

Eileen Bahring Sullivan
Columbia, South Carolina

When Grandmother's Lily Garden Blooms

Eileen Bahring Sullivan explains, "The inspiration for this quilt came from viewing a small bed of day lilies in the backyard – these wonderful flowers had been a favorite of mine for many years. It was with a 'piecer's eye' that I began to dissect the flower, with many variations in size, angle, etc."

Although Eileen began quilting with an interest in appliqué, she says that her main interest now is in developing pieced designs. She comments, "This quilt represented a great challenge.

first place

1990 AQS Show & Contest
Innovative Pieced, Pro

Finding a technique to bring this quilt to life opened a whole new chapter for me in quilting. I refused to give up the idea of piecing what I wanted to represent, and found myself drawing upon many possible techniques, and combining them, to make it a reality. This reaching and stretching has opened up the possibility of creating images with fabric that previously were only fleeting visions."

Eileen continues, "I developed a 'sew and flip' technique using a freezer paper foundation to eliminate the need for individual templates. It is an expansion of what we know as 'string piecing,' incorporating various shapes rather than strings. The units of the quilt are hexagons, which facilitated the piecing of each flower."

Speaking of her background, Eileen says, "The formation of a friendship quilt group in the small New England town where we were living in the late 1970's was my first exposure to quilting. One quilt was produced each month by the twelve of us. Many of the members continued on with their own work after the group ended. Quiltmaking offers me the ultimate opportunity to combine my art background and a lifelong interest in needlework for a new mode of artistic expression."

Asked if completing this quilt has had any effect on her life, Eileen comments, "Completing it resulted in my being a year older without really knowing what else happened that last year! Most of my previous work had been smaller in size, usually in the wall quilt category. At present I am continuing to use this new piecing technique alone and in combination with other techniques."

About the popularity of quilting, Eileen says, "Quiltmaking has universal appeal. It can be restful, rewarding, challenging, or dynamic, depending upon the individual involved. Quilters quickly come to realize how much there still is to try, to learn, and to enjoy."

Photo: Renee Ittner-McManus/The State, Columbia, SC.

"To have ventured into new territory with this quilt and had it so well received gave new life to the future quiltmaking held for me."

WHEN GRAND-
MOTHER'S
LILY GARDEN
BLOOMS
64" x 85"
©1990
Eileen Bahring
Sullivan

Museum of AQS Collection

Barbara Oliver Hartman
Flower Mound, Texas

Fuego En La Noche

Barbara Oliver Hartman says of her background, "About 1980 I began teaching myself to quilt. By 1985, I had completed many quilts, mostly inspired by Amish quilts, and begun to design on my own." Barbara adds, "Quilts are now my business. I teach and lecture as well as publish a pattern line. I also complete about five or six quilts each year."

second place

1990 AQS Show & Contest Innovative Pieced, Pro

FUEGO EN LA NOCHE is totally made of cotton fabric, with cotton batting. It is machine pieced and hand quilted, and the borders are painted. Barbara talks of selecting and creating fabrics for this quilt: "When selecting the fabric for this quilt, I

decided each fabric used would have to have black in it. If I wanted a certain color and it was not available with black, I painted it." Barbara adds, "Many of the colored circles in the quilt were painted on black fabric."

About her development as a quiltmaker, Barbara says, "Every quilt I make is a growing experience. Each one leads to the next, and even though the new may be different from the last, the process is cumulative."

Barbara says of the effect of winning this AQS award, "When Show Chair Klaudeen Hansen called me Tuesday evening to tell me I had won, I was so excited I could hardly sleep. My friends and I were leaving the next morning. I drove the whole way from Dallas to Paducah, talking non-stop. I was probably quite obnoxious. My friends were patient and kind."

Asked to comment on the current popularity of quilting, Barbara says, "Quilts remind people of a simpler time. Not only is the fabric soft and comforting, but many times quilts and their fabrics remind us of special people or special times in our lives. "

*"Quiltmaking as an art form is in its infancy;
I find it very exciting to be involved."*

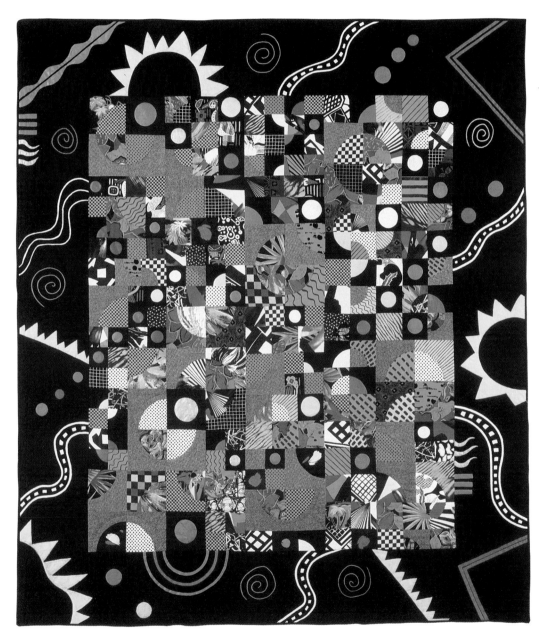

FUEGO EN
LA NOCHE
76" x 88"
1990
Barbara Oliver
Hartman

Katie Pasquini-Masopust
Santa Fe, New Mexico

Labyrinth

Katie Pasquini-Masopust explains, "This quilt was inspired by a book on isometric perspective published by Dover Publications. I was taken by the possibilities the isometric unit offered." Constructed of cottons, blends, and lamé, the quilt is hand and machine pieced, and hand quilted.

third place

1990 AQS Show & Contest Innovative Pieced, Pro

Katie comments, "I have always been drawn to geometric designs, and have worked with them since I first began quilting, generally in combination with bright colors and black. The top of this quilt is actually a composite of three design layers. I especially like the way the bright fabrics stand out against the black in the finished quilt. There are actually over 200 little isometric blocks in the black background. I really enjoyed working with many different black fabrics to create a rich texture."

Speaking of her quilting experience, Katie explains, "I began quilting in 1975 when I took what I thought was an embroidery class. The class turned out to involve more quilting than embroidery, but I loved it. Later I took several workshops from Michael James, and continued on to make art quilts."

Asked if she had come from a sewing background, Katie explains, "I was a painter. I worked with oils, using very thick paint to create texture. My father and older brother painted and encouraged me in my work. My mother sewed, but it was my sister who was encouraged to be the seamstress in our family."

Katie continues, "When I began making quilts after my class, I started making bed quilts. Then I tired of that and wanted to use my quilts as an expression of my art. I don't have a degree in art, but I have taken a lot of art courses and have been painting since I was about six years old. I found I really liked quilting – I liked expressing ideas in fabric. I really enjoy the fabrics – the colors and the textures."

Katie has been teaching quilting for about 12 years. She comments, "Much of what I do, I do intuitively. When I teach, I find I have to figure out how I do it. The teaching really helps me define my techniques. And out of that definition usually grows a book."

Asked if she would do anything differently if she were making the quilt now, Katie says she remains very happy with this quilt, but she adds, "It was done on a very tight deadline so maybe the change I would make would be to allow more time so I could complete the quilting stress free."

Responding to a question about possible reasons for the great popularity quilting is enjoying today, Katie says, "Quilting is a very tactile experience which involves many wonderful steps to complete the piece – choices of design, fabrics, color, techniques, quilting pattern, etc. All in all, making a quilt is a very satisfying experience."

"I really enjoy making quilts, and find it's more fun to take chances than to go along with the mainstream."

LABYRINTH
90" x 85"
1989
Katie Pasquini-
Masopust

Collection of
Bob Masopust, Sr.

Jennifer Patriarche
Dallas, Texas

Iris Germanica

Jennifer Patriarche says her quilt began with the purchase of the green background fabric from a shop holding an after-Christmas sale. She explains, "I bought the fabric and then had to do something with it. Since I have always loved flowers and irises in particular, IRIS GERMANICA was born. The title is the botanical name for the large showy irises that bloom in spring."

first place

1990 AQS Show & Contest
Appliqué, Amateur

Speaking of the development of the quilt, Jennifer says, "The iris blooms were almost all cut from a sampler package of 5" squares; only a few additional fabrics were used from my 'stash.' The leaves were cut from six different green fabrics ranging from light lime green to deep forest-green. A low loft batt was used."

About her background, Jennifer says, "Before I learned how to quilt, I did a great deal of knitting, smock-ing, and sewing, all good training in precision workmanship, use of color, and design. In 1981, we moved to a new city, and the time was just right to move to an art form that had fascinated me for years. It continues to enthrall me, and I know it always will. My quilts usually begin with a fabric I cannot resist, and quite often this fabric is green or purple."

Jennifer has her own method of quilt development. She discusses the making of this quilt: "I just designed the blocks, and then while stitching the blocks, developed the border design. At the time I was

Photo: Jim Patriarche

making the borders, I chose quilting patterns and made or bought stencils. I definitely don't have my quilts planned to the last stitch before I begin!"

Continuing, Jennifer adds, "I enjoy the planning stages as much as the sewing, so as I complete one stage I am having a wonderful time dreaming up what I will do next. I keep a notebook of grid paper and a pencil with me when I work. In fact, I almost always have the notebook and pencil with me, so I can jot down ideas, colors, architectural details – anything that might sometime be useful."

Asked about the impact of her American Quilter's Society show experience, Jennifer says that after that event, the design for this quilt was purchased by Better Homes and Gardens publishers, for inclusion in their book *America's Heritage Quilts*. She adds, "The award encouraged me to step into the world of teaching quilt-making – both appliqué and precision rotary cutting/ machine piecing. Teaching has been extremely reward-

"One of the great traditional arts, quilting links our generation with our grandmothers' – and hopefully with our granddaughters' too."

IRIS
GERMANICA
94" x 94"
1990
Jennifer
Patriarche

ing, and I continue to read and take courses myself to enlarge my own knowledge of quilting and to improve my own skills."

Jennifer feels quilting is popular in part because "It allows us to express our innermost selves, and develop our skills in the use of color, design, and form, while producing useful items of great beauty. It is the means of making great friendships."

Lorraine E. Simmons
Graham, Washington

Shalimar Garden

About SHALIMAR GARDEN Lorraine E. Simmons says, "I consider this quilt to be my masterpiece. It took two years of working five to six hours a day to complete it. When it was done I named it SHALIMAR GARDEN, in memory of my husband's and my honeymoon trip to Kashmir, Northern India. The lovely Shalimar Gardens are there, in the shadow of the Himalayas."

second place

*1990 AQS Show & Contest
Appliqué, Amateur*

Speaking of the development of the design, Lorraine explains, "I saw the quilt pictured on the cover of the book *American Patchwork Quilts,* published by the Spencer Museum of Art, University of Kansas. I developed the pattern from the photo, drafting one-quarter of the design and then repeating it around."

The quilt is constructed of all cotton materials, with a polyester batting, and is entirely hand stitched. Lorraine adds, "All of the feather designs are stuffed. For trapunto, I use yarn, after all of the quilting is finished."

Describing her background, Lorraine comments, "I began quilting about nine years ago. After loading my home with needlepoint pillows, embroidery, knitting, and crochet, I decided to try something else. Once I started quilting I was hooked. I have made pieced and appliquéd quilts, but I most enjoy appliqué. I have won ribbons every year at the Western Washington State

Fair and been Grand Champion twice. Completely self taught, I have read every book I could, but in spite of that I have also made many mistakes along the way."

Asked if she would do anything differently if beginning this quilt today, Lorraine says, "I would make smaller sections and then join them. I constructed the quilt in only four squares and it was difficult to handle because of all the close appliqué. Also, I would consider using more prints."

Lorraine has been affected by the completion of this quilt and the winning of this award: "I've had a great sense of accomplishment and pride. My husband is my greatest fan and booster, and at quilt shows I've had people remark that they saw the photo and name in *American Quilter* magazine."

About quilting and quilters, Lorraine says, "I have done all kinds of needlework and sewing since I was a child, but nothing equals quiltmaking. The quilters are all so very friendly and helpful to each other."

"Quilting has truly opened up a new life for me."

SHALIMAR
GARDEN
90" x 90"
1990
Lorraine E.
Simmons

Joan Rollins
Salt Lake City, Utah

Birds A-humming, Iris A-blooming

Asked how this quilt developed, Joan Rollins comments, "This quilt was inspired by an iris quilt made by Hannah H. Headlee of Kansas. I wanted to make the quilt she had made, but discovered the pattern was not available. Then Charlotte Warr Andersen, a friend of mine who designs her own quilts, made me realize I could design my own iris pattern."

third place

1990 AQS Show & Contest
Appliqué, Amateur

Discussing the design and construction, Joan says, "I designed this quilt when I had just learned the needle-turn appliqué technique. Because I was new at it, I didn't take into account the amount of detail involved in my design – the appearance was my priority." Joan adds, "Looking back, I would not even have started the project had I known what I was doing." Joan then adds, "The tailoring and sewing skills I'd developed over many years

and my recent instruction certainly paid off."

When asked if she would do anything differently if she were beginning the quilt today, Joan replies, "I would design the quilt and draw it full size rather than on an 8½" x 11" piece of paper. Then I could adapt it in its finished size. I would also organize my cut pieces better. With over 2,000 pieces, the quilt was hard to put together because the pieces were all mixed up. My being unorganized resulted in its taking me extra months to

complete the quilt."

Joan began quilting about 10 years ago when living in Virginia. She had visited a quilt shop, and then took beginning and intermediate classes. She comments, "I preferred doing appliqué, but I did not like the method that involved basting." She adds, "It wasn't until years later, when I was introduced to needle-turn methods, that I started to quilt again." Speaking of her quilting activity, Joan adds, "I also raise and show English Springer Spaniels and work full time as a graphic artist, so don't always have the time to quilt as much as I'd like to. I find quilting very relaxing."

Asked if the quilt or its award has had any impact on her life, Joan says, "It has brought the joy of knowing that my quilt is hanging in a prominent Utah home – that it will eventually be treasured by a descendant of that family or donated to a museum and that many people will view it as a piece of artwork."

About the popularity of quilting, Joan says, "Quilters see what they do as a love

"People who quilt love what they are doing and they are much fun to be around."

BIRDS
A-HUMMING,
IRIS
A-BLOOMING
61" x 81"
©1990
Joan Rollins

and a challenge. I think people who view these works are affected by this and are falling as much in love with quilting as the artists who quilt already are."

Linda Goodmon Emery
Derby, Kansas

Celtic Splendor

Speaking of the development of CELTIC SPLENDOR, Linda Goodmon Emery says, "I was intrigued with the idea of combining Celtic appliqué with patchwork. I enjoy working with a combination of techniques in the same quilt." This particular quilt combines Celtic appliqué, traditional appliqué and patchwork.

first place

1990 AQS Show & Contest
Appliqué, Pro

"CELTIC SPLENDOR," Linda continues, "began with the spark of an idea (the idea of combining Celtic appliqué and patchwork) – I had absolutely no idea what it would ultimately look like. I began sketching and it started taking shape. Then I decided to challenge myself by trying to color shade with purchased prints. This turned out to be the biggest challenge of the quilt. Once I had finally selected all my fabrics (about 75 different ones), the construction of the quilt was not overly difficult to complete."

Asked if she might change anything if she were beginning again, Linda comments that she might change the color scheme. She explains, "The colors I chose for my quilt were not the 'popular' colors available at the time. It would have been far easier to to have gone to quilt shops and used the most widely available and popular colors of the day – there would have been more variations to choose from."

Linda found her experience with this quilt satisfying: "Completing this quilt

satisfied my curiosity about making a successful quilt with the combination of techniques I had chosen. I felt very satisfied with its outcome. It was as though I had a mental list of things to try and this one could be marked off as accomplished!" She adds, "I enjoy intricate, time-consuming projects as well as the quick, small and 'fun' quilts. I began quilting in a very traditional manner, but soon found there were innumerable ideas I wanted to try. My current interest is in developing easier techniques and adding three-dimensional details."

About interest in quilting she says, "Interest in quilts has grown, I believe, because there is something for everyone in today's quiltmaking. Whether a person wants a small, easily accomplished project, an heirloom quilt, a personalized gift or a unique piece of clothing, it's available. Another very important factor is the wonderful time-saving methods and tools that are widely available, as well as help from a wide range of magazines, books and quilting classes."

"Quilting encompasses a vast area with unlimited possibilities for exploration – I never become bored with it."

CELTIC
SPLENDOR
73" x 87"
©1990
Linda
Goodmon
Emery

Rita Denenberg
Wellington, Florida

The Magic Flute

"THE MAGIC FLUTE," says Rita Denenberg, "is the result of imagination and lots of hard work and would have been unattainable without the assistance of a husband who took over household chores and encouraged me when I felt I had taken on too great an undertaking. When the fingers ached, and the eyes dimmed from strain, it was real nice to have someone say, 'You can do it!' "

second place

*1990 AQS Show & Contest
Appliqué, Pro*

The design was based on one of a set of Japanese figurines Rita and her husband own. Rita discusses the construction, "The quilt is composed mainly of chintz; each flower cluster is appliquéd with a minute buttonhole stitch, which people sometimes mistake for machine appliqué." She adds, "Each time the color in a flower or leaf changed, I changed embroidery floss to match, sometimes sewing only ⅛". After looking in six states for the right fabric for the flowers, I finally found it in a shop near my home!"

Of her background, Rita says, "I began quilting in 1983, after viewing Georgia Bonesteel on her PBS program. I have read quilt books and sewed constantly, completing at least ten bed quilts and various wallhangings since. I turned professional quilter in 1990, and presently lecture and hold workshops in quilting techniques."

Rita continues, "Every quilt has been a learning process for me – a challenge – and each quilt has been a labor of love and source of

joy! I learn to love this art more with each quilt, and with every quilt I admire I see how much more I want to do. I'm still in awe of this experience; the various awards I have received as a free-lance artist do not compare to those I receive as a quilter.

"Winning the award," says Rita, "has afforded me recognition and the opportunity to share my experiences and teach others this beautiful heritage. It has told me I'm heading in the right direction towards making a good quilt. It says I've learned my art well and encourages me to keep going, to try to be even better. An award such as this also brings one to one's knees, to say thank you to the Almighty for the gift."

About quiltmaking in general, Rita says, "Quilting, a tactile medium, has allowed me to paint with fabric. Making quilts requires more concentration and thought than other needlework activities, and allows me to be more creative. And my studies of the past histories of quilts and quilters have made me proud to be part of this rich heritage."

*"After the label, the last thing to be sewn on, has been attached
to a quilt I have made, I always feel that this quilt is the best I have done –
until the next one comes along."*

THE MAGIC
FLUTE
88" x 94"
©1989
Rita Denenberg

Mary Mashuta
Berkeley, California

Westward Ho!

WESTWARD HO!, one of Mary Mashuta's original story quilts, was inspired by a story she wrote in 1984. She explains, "WESTWARD HO! represents a childhood journey undertaken from New York to California. The time was shortly after World War II. The cast of characters included my 1940's pioneer-style parents, a gray Plymouth Coupe, and two five-year-old girls, carbon copies of each other. A sleek, streamlined trailer served as our Conestoga wagon.

third place

1990 AQS Show & Contest Appliqué, Pro

"Before our eyes a non-stop ribbon of asphalt unraveled. Other images blur, except those of giant rocks piled precariously like babies' blocks, and gargantuan cacti, their arms stretching skyward. Years later, we tried to determine how long this never-ending journey had actually lasted. In child time it seemed at least six months long. My mother, when closely questioned, said, 'Yes, it was a long time. I'm sure it took us at least six weeks!' "

Mary has been quilting since the early 1970's and has been a full-time professional since 1985. She currently lectures and teaches internationally, and has written two books: *Wearable Art for Real People* and *Story Quilts: Telling Your Tale in Fabric.*

WESTWARD HO! was constructed using traditional hand appliqué, raw edge machine appliqué, machine piecing, folded biscuit puffs, and folded origami puffs. It

was embellished with knots and photographs on fabric, and was hand quilted. Mary adds, "In addition to being a part of my on-going story quilt series, this quilt provided an opportunity to express what I have learned about the 'pushed-neutral' color scheme I invented. Basically, this approach to color involves learning how to use subtle, low-contrast colors in such a way that they still appear to have life in them. I consider this quilt my Master's thesis in pushed-neutrals."

About her award, Mary says, "Awards are only a bonus to me and not the reason I make quilts. I do hang my ribbons in my studio. I often spend prize money on my studio, but in this case, it probably went toward paying some bills, since I am a self-supporting professional."

Mary has these thoughts on the current popularity of quilting: "Fabric is non-threatening to women, unlike many other art media. Because there are so many different ways we can express ourselves in quilts – rather than just one way – it

46

*"I am pleased with the way this quilt came out.
Once a quilt is finished, it is finished as far as I'm concerned.
If I have more to say, I make another quilt."*

WESTWARD HO!
72" x 82"
1989
Mary Mashuta

allows for the development of the individual. This individual expression allows the movement to grow and change constantly rather than stagnate. This helps us to remain enthusiastic: there is always a new color, fabric, or technique to try."

Debra Wagner
Hutchinson, Minnesota

Ohio Bride's Quilt

Debra Wagner says that OHIO BRIDE'S QUILT contains quilting designs she found in various antique quilts. She looked at many quilts to collect designs she liked, particularly the urn patterns she occasionally found on quilts from Ohio.

first place

*1990 AQS Show & Contest
Other Techniques*

Debra used 100% cotton fabrics for the quilt. She assembled it without washing the cotton batting or backing, and then machine quilted the floral and feather design using 100% cotton machine embroidery thread for the quilting. Then she washed the entire quilt so that the back and batting would shrink enough to leave room for the trapunto. Polyester fill was added for the trapunto.

About her background, Debra says, "I've only been quilting for about five years, but have had a lifelong obsession with antique textiles, including quilts. My obsession goes beyond just owning or understanding antiques; I want to know what it is like to create the textile." She gives an example: "I would guess that I am the only person in the country who received a working copy of an antique spinning wheel for my high school graduation gift. (I know I was one of only two spinners in the entire county in which I lived. The other spinner was an elderly woman, a displaced person during WW II, who taught me to spin.) I learned to spin before the

summer was over, and was making yarn and knitting sweaters before the next spring. As I said earlier, I'm really obsessed!"

Debra continues, "Quilting was a natural step in my growing repertoire of textile techniques. Because of my background (a B.S. in clothing, textiles and design from the University of Wisconsin-Stout), I am well versed in hand stitching and embroidery – in fact, I am quite skilled – but I prefer to use the sewing machine. I've done machine embroidery since I was ten. I made money monogramming and name writing while I was in high school." Debra sums up her experience with machine work, "The sewing machine is like an extension of my hands. The machine makes it possible for me to quilt quickly and accurately."

In addition to quilting, Debra also spins and weaves, knits, crochets and does needlepoint. She makes lace, including bobbin lace, Battenburg lace and lace net darning on bridal illusion. She also does embroideries, including cutwork, Hardan-

"Because I am slightly color blind, subtle colors or illusions are lost on me. In my quilts, I prefer working with high contrast fabric combinations like primary solid or near solid colors with white or ivory."

OHIO BRIDE'S
QUILT
81" x 81"
1989
Debra Wagner

ger, and drawn thread work.

On the subject of the current popularity of quilting, Debra says, "I think part of the appeal of quiltmaking is in its extremes. On one end is the basic bed quilt – so simple it requires almost no sewing experience and can be completed in a day or two. On the other end are the intricate quilts that are art, not household linens. That range of skills and functions attracts many different people. Few textile arts offer as many skill levels or avenues of self expression."

Mary Crew
West Monroe, Louisiana

With Help From My Friends

Mary Crew explains that WITH HELP FROM MY FRIENDS is titled as it is because it includes not only her own designs, but also some developed by Marge Murphy, Pepper Cory, and Marianne Fons.

second place

*1990 AQS Show & Contest
Other Techniques*

Mary explains that after working out her overall design, she put it on heavy clear plastic so that she could keep it and not worry about its tearing. She then traced it onto her fabric. She adds, "I'm working on another whole-cloth quilt now, and the only difference is the design."

Asked about her background, Mary explains, "I started quilting in about 1974, when our first grandchild came along. About that time, Georgia Bonesteel's television shows began to be shown. I ordered her first book and made several quilts with her help. Then our first quilt shop opened, classes became available, and our local guild started." Now

quilting has become an important part of Mary's daily life.

Mary loves entering shows because she learns from the experience. She explains, "It keeps you trying to improve your work." About her award, she comments, "Winning this award has been the most thrilling thing that has ever happened to me. When you put your work into something and people who know about quilts say yours are good, there is no better feeling."

Mary adds, "I believe quilting is very popular because not only do we enjoy the work itself, but quilting is a very fulfilling craft. You meet and work with the best people in the world, you learn from each other, and you just plain have fun."

"I began quilting in about 1974, and now spend two to four hours each day doing it – quilting is my nerve tonic. "

WITH HELP
FROM MY
FRIENDS
85" x 94"
1989
Mary Crew

Mary E. Kuebler
Cincinnati, Ohio

Hawaii

Mary E. Kuebler says that even though this quilt won an award in the 1990 AQS Quilt Show and Contest, it was actually not completed until 1991. She explains, "I did much more quilting after the show, completely filling in the design. I quilted as if I were shading with a pencil."

third place

1990 AQS Show & Contest
Other Techniques

Mary comments on her inspiration for this quilt: "I had seen Hawaiian quilts featured in magazines and was fascinated, so I cut a pattern freely with paper and scissors and traced it. This design was the result." The quilt is constructed of a 100% cotton untreated sheet. The original design was traced and then batiked – the design was drawn in hot wax on the fabric and the fabric was then dyed in a bathtub with cold water Procion™ MX dyes, salt, and washing soda.

Speaking of her background in quilting, Mary says, "Twenty years ago I gave up knitting for quilting. My husband disliked the click of the needles." She continues, "I made an original appliqué, began piecing quilts, and then, as a result of an art class in batik, made my first 'big one,' a full-size bed batik that I quilted."

About her technique,

Mary says, "While quilting, I use neither frame nor hoop. In making this quilt, when my work had progressed to about a five-foot circle in the center of the piece, my left hand suddenly found a rip in the back. The fabric I had purchased was faulty, so I had to patch it. When I later showed this quilt at a guild show & tell, I showed the patch and explained what had happened. I added that the quilt could never be shown in a contest or competition of any kind as a result. A friend suggested I put my name plate over the patch. I did! Nothing is really perfect!"

Asked about the effect of her award, Mary says, "With the award money I was able to buy a piece of Carol Leibzeit's work. I'm very fond of her color interpretations." Mary adds, "The award night was fun. And, HAWAII was shown in Munich, Germany in 1992 in the American Haus, as part of the Sister City Project."

"Quilting, like art and music, is international and intersocial in nature, touching all people in one way or another."

HAWAII
82" x 86"
1991
Mary E.
Kuebler

Jane Holihan
Walworth, New York

Love Song

Jane Holihan says the 1990 AQS Quilt Show & Contest's fan theme was the inspiration for her quilt. She explains, "After researching many quilts and patterns in books and magazines, I decided to place the Fan pattern in the Carpenter's Wheel, and add a ribbon border."

first place

1990 AQS Show & Contest Theme: Fans

The quilt is pieced and appliquéd with cotton fabric, with a "touch of embroidery" added. Jane discusses the development of the quilt, "I began my quilt by purchasing the black flower print fabric. I appliquéd the center flowers to mirror the flowers in the border print."

"Every quilt I make seems to be a learning experience. I strive to do the very best I can in each one. Because I love nature, especially birds and flowers, I like to include a little bit of nature in each of my quilts."

Asked what she would most like people to know about this quilt, Jane replies, "I would like people to look at this quilt and to see all of its variety and detail."

Speaking about her background, Jane says, "I have always loved to sew. I began sewing in my early teens, and I became interested in quilting in the mid 1970's. I took my first quilting class at my home town library. Since

then I have taken several other classes to learn about color and various new quilting techniques."

About her award, Jane says, "Sometimes I feel that after quilting for so many years it might be time to go on to something else. Winning this award has made me realize that people enjoy my quilts, and it has given me the encouragement to continue quilting.

"I believe that interest in quilts and quiltmaking is so great because quilting is an art form through which women have expressed themselves for hundreds of years. While quilt styles are always changing, the tradition of quilting continues. Being involved in other art, craft, and needlework activities is different; through quilting I can express my love for sewing, art and nature all in one craft."

"I enjoyed making this quilt, and I don't think I would change anything about it."

LOVE SONG
88" x 88"
1989
Jane Holihan

Elsie Vredenburg
Tustin, Michigan

Ice Fantasia

The inspiration for this quilt by Elsie Vredenburg was the 1988 Winter Olympics figure skating competition and the 1990 AQS show theme – fans.

Asked what she would like people to know about this quilt, Elsie says, "A slip of the scissors isn't necessarily the end of the world. I cut the center too small in one direction. The solid color strips of the inner border were my solution for getting the people to fit evenly. If you look closely, you'll see they're different lengths on the ends than on the sides."

second place

1990 AQS Show & Contest Theme: Fans

Elsie adds, "Sometimes a mistake can be the creative nudge I need. I know not everyone likes that part of the quilt, but to me it adds something that would otherwise have been lacking."

Speaking of her background in quilting, Elsie says, "About 1958 my grandmother was living with us and

thought I should learn to quilt. Since I had begun at age 14, sewing had been my first love. For many years, I made nearly all of my family's clothes. After my children had grown up, I went back to quilting; the 1976 Bicentennial gave me a push."

Asked if she would do anything differently if beginning today, Elsie says, "I might take some classes. There weren't any when I began quilting. Today there are so many ideas, techniques, and great quilts. It's mind boggling." Elsie adds,

"I'm glad I learned early and worked on technique before I began getting 'great' ideas. I can create without having to learn the basic technique first." Elsie says her award has encouraged her to "stretch a bit more – to be much more willing to take a few risks."

Elsie believes the current popularity of quilting is due in part to "our increasingly technical and impersonal society." She explains, "Quilting offers women the sense of community that was provided in earlier days by extended families and closely knit communities." Elsie continues, "Even though I work alone, I need the stimulus of my quilt group, the sense of belonging, the approval, the encouragement they provide. Why are quilts so different in this respect from other arts/crafts – I think there are a number of reasons. Did you ever try to comfort a child by wrapping him in a painting? Can you achieve the same variety of expression with a knitted design as you can with a quilt?"

Continuing, Elsie says, "Quilting does it all, and yet

"I'll never be an 'art' quilter, but this quilt and its award have encouraged me to venture out of the 'safe' world of purely traditional quilts and do something more unique."

ICE FANTASIA
74" x 89"
©1989
Elsie
Vredenburg

Museum of AQS Collection

primarily uses only basic sewing skills within the grasp of most people. A quilt can be as utilitarian as old clothing pieced together to make a warm covering, or as lofty as a great work of art, as crude or elegant as the materials and techniques used."

Sheri Wilkinson Lalk
Electra, Texas

Fanciful Garden

Speaking of the development of FANCIFUL GARDEN, Sheri Wilkinson Lalk says, "When I heard about the 1990 AQS Quilt Show theme – fans – I started thinking about all of the many possibilities it offered me as a quilter. I would close my eyes and see fan flowers 'vining' and swirling around."

third place

1990 AQS Show & Contest Theme: Fans

Sheri continues, "I love to appliqué, so I thought that appliqué would be the best way for me to create the design I wanted. I used 100% cotton fabric because that works the best for curved appliqué pieces. I chose shades of green, pink, yellow, peach, blue and purple. I like to use many different fabrics to make a more interesting design."

Elaborating on the development of this quilt, Sheri explains, "I wanted the appliqué in this quilt to 'vine' and grow like real flowers. I didn't want to have one flower on one side and one on the other side in the exact same place. I wanted the design to look more natural and not so calculated." Sheri adds, "I like to do freestyle quilting, too."

Speaking of her background, Sheri comments, "I started quilting about ten years ago. I have always been interested in creating things, and have always done some type of needlework and crafts. I enjoy making my own designs." She adds, "I'm always designing new ideas. I hope I will have enough time to make everything I want to make. Everywhere I look I find another idea. And there is so little time!"

Asked about her response to winning an award, Sheri says, "I was very shocked when I got the call saying I had won. It was the first time I had ever entered a quilt in a national show. I am still amazed when I consider how many beautiful quilts there were in the show. So many really good quilts don't even get ribbons. I felt very honored. I still get a thrill when I open the show issue of *American Quilter* magazine and see my quilt there."

"I think people love to create something with their own hands, whether it's quilts or crafts."

FANCIFUL
GARDEN
70" x 85"
1990
Sheri
Wilkinson Lalk

Patricia B. Campbell
Dallas, Texas

Jacobean Arbor

Asked how she became involved in quilting, Pat Campbell says, "Bored with needlepoint and knitting, I took my first quiltmaking class in 1983. My plan was to make a Victorian crazy quilt.

first place

*1990 AQS Show & Contest
Group/Team*

I was immediately 'hooked' on quilts and took every class offered in my area. One year later I began teaching hand appliqué; it had become a passion. I now stitch three to five hours each day, and feel as if something is missing if I don't pick up my needle. I never did make that crazy quilt, but I now own four that are over a hundred years old."

JACOBEAN ARBOR is constructed of 100% cotton fabrics and a few bits of silk. The hand appliquéd shapes are cut from a selection of commercially printed quilting fabrics, combined with several commercially produced hand-dyed fabrics and a few "fashion fabrics."

Speaking of this quilt, Pat says, "My inspiration came from seventeenth century crewel embroidery motifs. The quilt represents a part of me – my love for flowers and color." Pat adds, "I feel one should make a statement in a quilt, through the design, the color, or the story."

Asked if she would do anything differently if she were beginning the quilt today, Pat replies, "I would not change this quilt. I take it to all my show and guild engagements and it still gets 'oohs' and 'aahs!' It touches my heart."

Pat adds, "The blue ribbon at the 1990 AQS Show and having my quilt on the cover of *American Quilter* magazine put my name in lights! I now travel to teach about every two weeks for major quilt shows and guilds across the country. And this past year my teaching included a trip to South Africa!"

Asked to comment on the popularity of quilting today, Pat says, " 'Crafty' ladies were looking for something different. Quilts give them the solace and enjoyment of stitching, as well as the friendship of guilds and shows. All of these bring out their creativity."

"I had always admired the 'botanical fantasies' found in seventeenth century needlework, and felt they could be translated to fabric."

JACOBEAN
ARBOR
80" x 80"
©1989
Patricia B.
Campbell

Quilted by
Jackie
Muehlstein

Mary Klett Ryan & Jan Snelling
Rutland, Vermont

Paramount Stars

PARAMOUNT STARS is constructed of 100% cottons, using a variety of techniques including machine piecing, quick cutting, quick piecing, appliqué, and hand quilting. Mary Ryan, designer of this quilt, comments, "The Feathered Star is a design I love, and the medallion setting offers quiltmakers a wonderful opportunity to create many different elements within a single quilt."

second place

1990 AQS Show & Contest Group/Team

Mary explains that she designed the quilt in response to a local group's request for a quilt to raffle for funds to restore a theater. She describes the project, "Thirty members of our Maple Leaf Quilters made the first version of this quilt in thirty days. It was machine quilted and presented to the Paramount Center."

The quilt design was then modified. Mary explains, "As a proposal for the Vermont Quilt Festival raffle quilt, the design was made more complex. The appliqué border was softened: half-square triangle or Sawtooth borders replaced whole-cloth strips, Eight Point Stars replaced quick-pieced stars, and hand quilting by Cyndy Gates added beautiful dimension to the design."

About winning the award, Mary says, "It was a complete surprise and pleasure to win the award, especially since there were three of us to share the honors. The quilt has been published in *American Quilter* magazine and used in Fairfield Processing Corporation's 1991 holiday advertising campaign. Quiltmakers around the country have been in touch with us because of this quilt."

Asked about her background in quilting, Mary says, "I had never seen a real quilt before I took my first class in 1974, although I had been fascinated with the quilts featured in home decorating magazines. In 1979 a week-long seminar with Beth Gutcheon at Vassar College helped me realize I could incorporate in my quilt designs the paisleys and bor- der prints I had loved for years. I was off and running." Speaking of her own background, Jan Snelling says, "I have been quilting since 1974 and continue to be as excited about quiltmaking as I was when I started."

Both Mary and Jan have much to say about the current popularity of quilting. Jan comments, "It offers an opportunity for personal expression that you cannot find in other needlework forms. Several years ago I started making quilts with Mary Ryan. Collaborating with another quiltmaker is an experience I would recommend. Our friendship has become more special because of our quilting connection."

Mary comments: "I wholeheartedly concur with Jan about collaborating! We collaborate on many quilts, but Jan creates her own quilts also, specializing in Japanese patchwork. I specialize in quilts based on Islamic designs, and in quilts using border prints and other exotic fabrics. Quilting is a broad art with a niche for everyone. It offers a release for the creativity in each of

Mary Ryan comments: "Quilts, because of their color, texture, design – and warmth and comfort – draw us into them. What other art show needs to have 'do not touch' signs?"

PARAMOUNT
STARS
96" x 96"
©1990
Mary Klett
Ryan
& Jan Snelling

Quilted by
Cyndy Gates

us, and with minimum instruction, even a beginner can achieve wonderful results. "

Nancy Johnson-Srebro & Debbie Grow
Tunkhannock, Pennsylvania

Wyoming

Commenting on the development of this quilt, Nancy Johnson-Srebro says, "I'd been working with miniature quilts for two years and wondered what a full size quilt made from miniature pieces would look like. This quilt is totally machine sewn with ¼" seam allowances, even the miniature bear's paws."

third place

1990 AQS Show & Contest Group/Team

Nancy Johnson-Srebro began doing the actual quilting process in 1984. She adds, "In 1988 I had wrist operations for carpal tunnel syndrome. I do very little quilting now."

Debbie Grow was first introduced to quilting in 1976. She comments, "I was immediately hooked! I was basically self taught; then I met Nancy. She helped me perfect my sewing skills. We laugh at how I turned out only one so-so quilt a year, until we got together! My real passion besides actually

quilting is appliqué."

There are many things Nancy Johnson-Srebro would like people to know about this quilt. She began the project while her husband and two sons drove to Wyoming. She adds, "Little did my husband realize that when he returned I would be knee-deep in miniature Bear's Paws! There are over six thousand pieces in this quilt, and a total of four hundred forty miniature Bear's Paws." Nancy adds, "I want people to realize that you can successfully use miniature pieces in full-size quilts."

WYOMING was the first

quilt Nancy and Debbie entered in competition. They comment, "We decided to enter a slide of this quilt top in a national show. We didn't really think it would be accepted. We were accepted and the quilt had to be quilted in six weeks. From that time on, we have never entered a show without having the quilt finished!" Debbie adds, "This quilt is the result of a very special friendship. There were lots of laughs and tears, so it was especially thrilling to learn we had been recognized with the award."

About quiltmaking, Nancy

Left: Nancy Johnson-Srebro, right: Debbie Grow

Nancy Johnson-Srebro: "My thirst for new designs and techniques will never be quenched as long as 100% cotton fabric exists."

WYOMING
74" x 87"
©1989
Nancy
Johnson-Srebro
& Debbie Grow

says: "People are looking for an art form that will help them reduce the stress in their lives – and quiltmakinq does it." Debbie adds, "I think quilts have the power to touch our lives in a totally different way than any other craft does!"

Mary Kay Hitchner
Haverford, Pennsylvania

Tulips Aglow: 1830's Revisited

"TULIPS AGLOW: 1830'S REVISITED," says Mary Kay Hitchner, "is part of a group of quilts that reflect my interest in antique quilts. After selecting a time period, I research styles, patterns, and colors popular during that time and use this information as a starting point for designing a quilt."

best wall quilt

1990 AQS Show & Contest

Speaking of the quilt's development, she says, "My goal was to capture the feeling or mood of the period while using contemporary fabrics." She continues, "This machine-pieced and hand-quilted wallhanging features the classic medallion style popular in the 1830's and many other popular design characteristics: a Feathered Star centered with whirling tulips; borders of Sawtooth triangles and Nine-Patch blocks set on-point. The outside border is a flower (tulip) repeat-stripe fabric that is also used in the star center. Although the colors are quite vivid individually (and not necessarily 1830's colors), together they mellow to a muted 1830's look."

Of her background, Mary Kay says, "I began making patchwork pillows in 1970 and moved into quiltmaking from there. I make all types of quilts – traditional, contemporary, and somewhere in-between. It used to bother me that I didn't develop a recognizable style. I now realize that that has allowed me the freedom to do anything I want and concentrate on what I really love, which is working on unusual combinations of fabrics to achieve the look I want for each quilt."

About TULIPS AGLOW: 1830'S REVISITED, May Kay says, "The central Feathered Star block was made as a visual aid for a book review given to my quilt guild. Unable to copy anything – I have this innate urge to change things so mine is different – the block only remotely resembles the original in the book. I showed it anyway, pointing out what you can't do with fast-cut/fast-piece methods; special effects such as the radiance can't be cut and pieced in a random fashion."

Asked if she would change anything if making this quilt now, Mary Kay replies, "No. Although this was the most traditional quilt I had made in years and I considered it a step backwards in my design development, I found I loved the color exercise."

About her award, Mary Kay says, "The AQS award has brought invitations to exhibit my quilts in quilt shows and art museums."

"Whatever our serious interest, be it sports, gardening, music, or quilting, we have a desire for total immersion. It is just human nature to want more and more of what we love!"

TULIPS AGLOW:
1830'S
REVISITED
54" x 54"
1989
Mary Kay
Hitchner

Museum of AQS Collection

Donna French Collins
Bridgeport, New York

Baltimore Album Beauty

This quilt, which was later renamed PETITE BALTIMORE by its maker, Donna French Collins, was inspired by Elly Sienkiewicz's first book, *Spoken Without a Word: A Lexicon of Selected Symbols with 24 Patterns from Classic Baltimore Album Quilts.* Donna explains, "I miniaturized the patterns and made them into a quilt." She continues, explaining that she used needle-turn appliqué, and that all of the fabrics used were hand dyed by Edith Tanniru of American Beauty fabrics.

first place

1990 AQS Show & Contest Wall Quilt, Amateur

Speaking of her background, Donna says, "I began quilting about six years ago. I've always liked doing hand crafts. One day I met a woman who quilted and immediately fell in love with quilting. Since that time quilting has taken priority over all other activities, except my husband Michael and my daughters Kelly and Kimber. Now I design my own patterns and quilts."

About BALTIMORE ALBUM BEAUTY, Donna says, "This quilt took longer to complete from start to finish than any other quilt I've made. I really enjoyed working in miniature and with the fabric, and when I finished the quilt I felt as if I had given birth to my third child." Asked if she would do anything differently if she were beginning the quilt now, she says, "No, I would use the same technique and the same fabric."

Donna comments on her award, "I was thrilled to be accepted into the AQS show and overwhelmed when I won. I have learned much by entering contests; I don't think I would be where I am today if I didn't have the courage to enter shows and I didn't have the support of my family and friends."

Asked why she feels quilting is so popular today, Donna replies, "Quilts are not only beautiful and unique, but also enjoyable to make. Many quilts take you back in history, some make statements, and others are just for fun. Quilts let you express yourself in many ways, unlike most other crafts, which are limited. Quilts to me mean love, warmth, friendship and sharing all rolled up into one beautiful package."

"The AQS award helped me realize how much other people appreciate my work, which in turn has made me proud to share it."

BALTIMORE
ALBUM BEAUTY
45" x 45"
1989
Donna French
Collins

Nancy S. Brown
Oakland, California

The Animal Alphabet Quilt

Nancy S. Brown explains that this original design "was really inspired by some fabric." She continues, "Before making this quilt I had made a few others, using solid fabrics only. When I found some prints that looked like fur, sky, water, trees, grass, etc., I thought I would give them a try. Since I wanted to include several animals in different backgrounds, I thought that an animal alphabet quilt would pull them together."

second place

1990 AQS Show & Contest Wall Quilt, Amateur

The animals in the resulting wall quilt were hand appliquéd and quilted, and some of the finer details, such as the eyes, were embroidered. Nancy adds, "Most people don't know that this quilt is completely reversible. Behind each animal block is a block with the name of the animal and its alphabet letter. The front and back blocks weren't difficult to match because the blocks were lap quilted and then pieced together by machine." She also reveals that the border pattern was quilted from the back because the black fabric was easier to mark than the black and white.

Speaking of her background, Nancy says, "My mother taught me to quilt about ten years ago, after she had taken a class. I liked the idea of being able to create a large design without having

to have a large amount of room to do it in, and I also liked the idea that a quilt might last a long time."

About her award Nancy says, "After seeing the quality of the quilts in an AQS show for the first time that year, I felt very honored that my quilt had been accepted and a bit overwhelmed that it had actually won an award." Asked if she would do anything differently now, Nancy says, "I would much rather learn from my mistakes and make a quilt with a new design than repeat a quilt I have already made. In this quilt the backgrounds in some blocks could have been better colors, so the animal could be more easily seen, but for the most part I'm happy with the quilt."

Commenting on the popularity of quiltmaking, Nancy says, "I think that quiltmaking is very popular because the possibilities for creativity are endless, the process is very enjoyable, and the people involved are very friendly and supportive."

"The AQS show award didn't change how or why I quilt, but it certainly was encouraging to receive a pat on the back!"

THE ANIMAL
ALPHABET
QUILT
41" x 57"
1989
Nancy S. Brown

Pat Magaret
Pullman, Washington

Carnation Carousel

Speaking of the development of her quilt, Pat Margaret says, "CARNATION CAROUSEL was inspired by a Judy Martin quilting design shown in the May 1987 issue of *Quilter's Newsletter Magazine*. I adapted the lines for use as an appliqué design."

third place

1990 AQS Show & Contest Wall Quilt, Amateur

Pat continues, "The wall-hanging was made as part of a quilter's challenge. Those who participated were given a predetermined packet of fabrics. We could add several of our own choosing and eliminate one. I love appliqué, particularly when combined with pieced work. The combination of curved and straight lines is very pleasing to me. The project went smoothly until I had to decide how to quilt it. I fretted over this design aspect for several weeks. One day, it all came together. Creativity can't be rushed.

"Construction of the quilt," explains Pat, "took 149½ hours and involved several techniques. It was machine pieced, hand appliquéd and hand quilted. In addition, the center of the carnation wreath contains trapunto and stipple quilting." Pat adds, "Judges repeatedly comment that the piece would have benefited had I done more trapunto in the flower petals and leaves and between the circular quilting motifs. I had originally planned on using trapunto in those areas, but my experience with this technique proved frustrating, so I

couldn't face doing any more. Now I wish I had been more persistent."

About her background, Pat says, "I finished my first quilt in 1982, after several years of extensive reading and studying. My interest evolved slowly; I can't put my finger on any one thing that triggered it. My mother taught me to make doll clothes, and then clothes for myself, but she never mentioned quilts. The skills I learned from her, from 4-H, and from high school home economics all made quilting a 'natural' once I became interested. Now, my mother is starting to get 'the bug.' Hopefully, it is my turn to share with her."

Of her award, Pat says, "Winning this award was a great joy and a tremendous surprise. Since then, CARNATION CAROUSEL has won other awards, its photo has been published several times and it has seen more of the United States than I have. All this has proved to me that even 'everyday quilters' can make quilts of merit. I hope others will be encouraged to share their quilts. Nothing

"I have found that belonging to quilt groups can be a wonderful learning and sharing experience. This quilt was part of a quilter's challenge for the Palouse Patchers of Moscow, Idaho."

CARNATION
CAROUSEL
40" x 40"
1989
Pat Magaret

can happen if they aren't willing to take the risk of filling out an entry form and subjecting their quilts to the judges' scrutiny."

Speaking of interest in quilting, Pat comments, "When quilts were hung on walls as well as laid on beds, the world began to recognize them as an art form. This was the beginning of today's quilt and quiltmaking revival. We all need a release from our hectic schedules. Quilting allows us to make something that is not only lovely, but also useful. I believe this dual aspect of quilting has made it a popular pastime. We like to feel we are accomplishing several things at one time, yet enjoying every minute of it."

Agnes Holbrook Jevne
Escondido, California

Reflections

Speaking of her background in quilting, Agnes Holbrook Jevne says, "Prior to taking a class from Ruth Briggs in 1983, I had not been exposed to any quilting other than trying a couple of projects on my own. In 1984 I learned the freezer paper appliqué technique from Anne Oliver, and that opened new avenues for me."

first place

1990 AQS Show & Contest Wall Quilt, Professional

About this quilt's inspiration, Agnes says, "The silhouette on a Hallmark greeting card seemed to lend itself to working the reverse appliqué technique which is one of my favorites. I could immediately see how to reproduce the design in a quilt, and I knew I would enjoy working with the intricate trees.

"I used freezer paper for my drawing and a light box, which is indispensable for any appliqué. Using reverse appliqué on a whole-cloth quilt is a technique I devised myself. I find it a fascinating way to appliqué. The whole front of the quilt inside of the borders was cut from one piece of fabric and was drawn as a single image on several pieces of freezer paper taped together.

"Using the freezer paper drawing and the light box, I drew the image onto the front fabric, then cut away around it to reveal the background." Agnes adds, "If I were beginning this quilt today, with the experience I have gained, I would have used my own design rather than one found on a greeting card."

Agnes says of her award: "Winning the award for this quilt has brought me the respect of my peers, which means a great deal to me. I feel I have a God-given talent, and making quilts is a gift. Each award gives me great satisfaction."

Of her background, Agnes says, "My husband, who is my biggest fan, and I will be celebrating our 40th wedding anniversary in 1992. We have two daughters, one son and five grandchildren. My oldest daughter, Kathy Jevne Clark, is also a very accomplished quilter and has won many awards for her quilts. We share and enjoy quilts together, even though we have to do it long distance."

Agnes adds, "I think all quilters are nice people and being involved with them gives me great satisfaction. Interest in quilts remains strong because of the satisfaction and enjoyment involved, whether you're a lone sewer or a social person. There is something for everyone regardless of age, race, or economic status."

"Taking different classes in the early 1980's, I discovered I preferred appliqué because of its great versatility. There were very few appliqué teachers then, so I had to do a lot of improvising."

REFLECTIONS
53" x 65"
1989
Agnes
Holbrook Jevne

Caryl Bryer Fallert
Oswego, Illinois

High Tech Tucks #17

Caryl Bryer Fallert says that for as long as she can remember, she has been expressing herself through artwork. About her involvement with quiltmaking she says, "I began quilting after seeing quilts made by an 80-year-old woman in Missouri. My first quilts were traditional; I began making 'art quilts' in 1983."

second place

1990 AQS Show & Contest Wall Quilt, Professional

HIGH TECH TUCKS #17, which now hangs in the world headquarters of the Bernina Sewing Machine Company in Switzerland, incorporates several techniques Caryl has developed. To construct the quilt, she pieced the background, cut it into strips, and then reassembled the parts, with a tuck added to each seam allowance. The fabrics were all hand dyed by Caryl, and each tuck is made of two different fabrics.

Speaking about the quilt's development, Caryl explains, "HIGH TECH TUCKS #17 is part of an ongoing series in which I am experimenting with texture and color relationships. The pieced background is composed of only black, white, and gray, and the tucks are gradations of color. The twisting of the tucks and the differences in color and value create an illusion of movement and luminescence. The radiating string-pieced border is designed to draw the eye inward, toward the light at the center of the quilt."

She explains, "The focus of my work is on the qualities of color, line and texture that will engage the spirit and emotions of the viewer, evoking a sense of mystery, excitement, or joy. Each piece includes multiple levels of visual activity, often with illusions of movement and light. Textures created by layering, pleating, and quilting invite the viewer to touch as well as to look." She adds, "Though my quilts are inspired by life experiences, they are abstract, and are really more about seeing, experiencing, and imagining than about pictorial representation of any specific object or species."

Asked why she thinks quilting has enjoyed such popularity, Caryl replies, "I have worked with the public for 23 years, and the people I have met through quilting have been the warmest, and most creative people. I have not found this warmth and friendliness among any other group. I have no idea why it is this way, but I feel very lucky to be involved."

"It is very important to me that my work speaks to others, delighting the eye, or lifting the spirits of those who see it. An award lets me know that with this quilt I have been successful in meeting that goal."

HIGH TECH
TUCKS #17
53" x 56"
1989
Caryl Bryer
Fallert

Mary Morgan
Little Rock, Arkansas

Ebb & Flow II

Speaking of her background, Mary Morgan says, "I used to sew clothing for my two daughters and enjoyed that, but in the early 1970's they reached the point where they wanted to wear jeans and other purchased clothing. I had been thinking about making a quilt – I had reached the point where I needed a creative outlet. My first quilt was an all white

third place

*1990 AQS Show & Contest
Wall Quilt, Professional*

whole-cloth quilt. I didn't think I could sew a lot of little pieces together, so a whole-cloth quilt seemed to be the easiest kind of quilt to make. Little did I know. The quilt took two years to complete and was not very good."

Mary Morgan dyes all of her own fabrics. She says of this quilt, "The fabrics in EBB & FLOW II are all hand-dyed cottons; the stripe is an over-dyed black and white stripe. This machine pieced and quilted quilt is really very simple in pattern – it's composed of just a solid square alternating with a two-triangle square. The color changes are what create interest and excitement." After she had been dyeing fabrics for a while, Mary took a workshop with Jan Myers Newbury, from whom she learned much. Mary comments, "My work has been and still is highly influenced by her. "

Mary remains very happy with this quilt, and enjoyed winning the award. She doesn't, though, feel as if the award has had a tremendous effect on her life. It has just made her feel good.

Asked about today's strong interest in quilts and quilting, Mary comments, "I feel divided about the interest. On the one hand, quilting is more popular than other crafts and more mainstream. But, on the other hand, when it comes to selling quilts as works of art, we still have a long way to go. Artists in general have a hard time. And craftspeople have an even harder time selling their work. And I think quilters are at the bottom of the line for craftspeople. That may be because we haven't been around long enough to really become accepted. Although respect for quilts is growing, many top art museums still do not show them or show them infrequently."

A founder and current member of the Arkansas Quilter's Guild, Mary says her quilting group is very important to her. It offers both fellowship and validation. She adds, "It's fun being around people who share the same interest and who appreciate what I do. "

"I like to keep the pattern simple and rely on color changes for interest and excitement."

EBB & FLOW II
62" x 62"
1989
Mary Morgan

Adabelle Dremann
Princeton, Illinois

Corn Crib

Adabelle Dremann's quilt CORN CRIB was not based on a pattern or influenced by another quilt. Rather, she explained, "This crib could be seen from our back door. The pattern of farm machinery seen through the corn crib, silhouetted against the sky, inspired me to draw it, then make an oil painting from the sketch. Years later, the sketch was used as the basis for this wall quilt. All of the design is original, created by me."

first place

1990 AQS Show & Contest Pictorial Wall Quilt

The quilt is constructed of all cotton quilt percales, and is hand-appliquéd, except for the long border strips, which were attached by machine.

Speaking of her background, Adabelle said, "I made my first quilt in 1934, and also made a baby crib quilt of nursery rhyme characters that year. Fifty years passed before I again made quilts, five of them. All of these quilts have been original appliqué, and all of them have hung in American Quilter's Society shows, in 1986, 1987, 1989, 1990, and 1992. Between the two periods I was quilting, I did farmwife things, cared for our children, and taught school. All

Adabelle Dremann
1910-1992

of that accounts for fifty very busy years."

Adabelle said there was nothing she would do differently were she beginning the quilt in 1992. She explained, "The quilt reflects my ideas and memories." About the effects of winning an award for the quilt, she commented, "Winning the AQS award reinforced my trust in my own judgement."

Asked why she felt there is such a strong interest in quilting today, Adabelle explained, "Quiltmaking is different from some other arts and crafts because you can do whatever you want, as long as you are able."

After Adabelle's death on October 27, 1992, her son, Gordon Dremann, spoke of his mother's great enjoyment of anything artistic, including quilting and painting, and her love for traveling. He added, "It's a shame she hadn't had enough time to put all of her many ideas into quilts."

Asked what she would most like people to know about this quilt, Adabelle Dremann said, "That it was made in memory of life many years ago on our farm."

CORN CRIB
42" x 47"
1989
Adabelle
Dremann

Museum of AQS Collection

Marguerite Ann Malwitz
Brookfield, Connecticut

Desert Sunrise: Desert Botanical Gardens

Marguerite Ann Malwitz says that DESERT SUNRISE "was initially inspired by a trip to the Desert Botanical Gardens in Phoenix, Arizona." She continues, "A secondary jolt of inspiration came from a trip to Santa Fe where I observed an art community that was not afraid to use color. Further inspiration came from a Bible verse, Isaiah 51:3: 'And her wilderness He will make like Eden, and her desert like the garden of the Lord.' The desert and cacti are recurring themes in my quilts and both continue to challenge my creativity and design direction."

second place

*1990 AQS Show & Contest
Pictorial Wall Quilt*

Speaking of her background, Marguerite comments, "I have a BA degree in art education and spent several years teaching art in public school. Later, with young children to raise, I set up a studio in my home. For many years I was a weaver executing large pictorial tapestry commissions. In 1985 I began quilting and gradually dropped my involvement with weaving."

Marguerite says her current quilts are "inspired by the American landscape." She explains, "In DESERT SUNRISE I had a real need to create a picture of a garden with a variety of images. The inner directive became 'just design it and get it together any way you can!' This continues to be the current approach to my quilt work, more of a pictorial collage approach which has brought me back to my roots as a pictorial tapestry weaver and as an art major who continues to love great scenic paintings. With this background, creating pictures in fabric was a natural course for my work to take." Asked if this quilt would be any different if she were making it now, Marguerite says, "It would be less literal, less controlled, less exacting, and more spontaneous."

Speaking of her work, Marguerite adds, "It is my objective as an artist to continue to see growth in my work, and to share my journey in quiltmaking with others through exhibitions, speaking, teaching, and writing." About the quilt world, she says: "Having been associated with the craft and art world for many years, I really do notice a difference when comparing the quilt world to other fields. There is a wonderful camaraderie, acceptance, and common ground that exists between quilters, no matter what the differences in style, ability, or achievement. I have not seen or experienced this in other craft fields! It is always a delight to meet, to know, and to have quilters as friends."

Photo: David Malwitz

82

"This quilt represented a major change in my work. With its design and construction, I left the safety of the repeat-block approach to making a quilt. It had ceased to be right for what I wanted to say."

DESERT
SUNRISE:
DESERT
BOTANICAL
GARDENS
41" x 53"
© 1990
Marguerite Ann
Malwitz

Suzanne Marshall
Clayton, Missouri

The Soul of Medieval Italy

Suzanne Marshall comments: "I started quilting around 1977 because our four children needed blankets for their beds. I had saved scraps of fabric from years of making clothes for myself and the children, so I thought it might be fun to use the scraps and make a quilt. At that time I didn't know anyone who made quilts, so I went to the public library, checked out a book, and got started."

third place

*1990 AQS Show & Contest
Pictorial Wall Quilt*

Suzanne continues, "When making this quilt, I really didn't know how to make appliquéd trees. I experimented with different ways to make them, which can be seen in the different squares of the quilt. In fact, I was doing lots of experimenting while making this quilt because at that time I hadn't had very much experience with appliqué."

Speaking about the development of this quilt, Suzanne explains, "In December of 1963 we received a *Natural History* magazine that contained an article called, 'A Medieval Codex of Italy.' It was about a manuscript of the *Tacuinum Sanitatis*, which is presently in the Spencer Collection of the New York Public Library. This manuscript was illustrated during the fifteenth century and was written in a northern Italian dialect.

"I was enchanted with the illustrations, which were simple drawings containing scenes of daily life. Unlike the illuminated manuscripts meant for the lord of the

manor and princes of the church, this manuscript dealt with subjects close to the average person. I was fascinated! For years, every time we moved or I felt the need to throw out old magazines, I kept this one.

"Nearly a quarter of a century later I thumbed through the magazine again and decided to attempt making a quilt by adapting some of the illustrations. My first try was the illustration on falconry. I liked it, so I kept going."

Suzanne comments on her award, "THE SOUL OF MEDIEVAL ITALY has brought lots of pleasant surprises to my life – especially winning an award in Paducah – something I had only *dreamed* of doing. The quilt also appears on the title page of a book and was included in a three-month exhibit at the Museum of American Folk Art in New York City in the spring of 1991 in conjunction with the publication of the book. My husband and I lived in New York City in the early 1960's as 'starving students.' Never did I imagine that I would someday actually have a quilt hanging in an exhibit at

84

"Our four children are grown up and living away from home now. It makes me feel good to know that they are sleeping under quilts that I have made for them."

THE SOUL OF
MEDIEVAL
ITALY
71" x 79"
1987
Suzanne
Marshall

a museum there."

Suzanne adds: "The month that I finished the quilt our teenage daughter, Melissa, learned that she would be an American Field Service student the following year in the same region of Italy in which the original manuscript had been written and illustrated. The quilt will eventually be hers."

Joan Rollins
Salt Lake City, Utah

Birds A-humming, Iris A-blooming

Speaking about her background, Joan Rollins comments, "I have always enjoyed hand work; I find it very relaxing. About ten years ago I visited a quilt shop in Occoquan, Virginia, and fell in love with the fabrics and samples that were hanging on the shop's walls. I took my first quilting class there." Joan continues, "My husband is in the Marine Corps, so I was only able to

first quilt award

1990 AQS Show & Contest

take two classes before he was transferred to San Clemente, California. There I worked in a fabric store that specialized in tailoring and I became more involved with that facet of sewing." Joan adds, "But I did start a collection of silks and unusual fabrics, which were later used in this quilt."

Joan continues, "I became involved in quilting again when my family moved from California to Salt Lake City, Utah. I was introduced to Charlotte Warr Andersen and

Jeana Kimball through a mutual friend. Through them, I realized that I could design my own quilts, which meant that I could make an iris quilt like Hannah H. Headlee's Iris Quilt even though no pattern was available." Speaking of the design development, Joan says, "Since I am an artist, I drew my own pattern for the iris quilt, developed my needle-turn appliqué skills through classes, and began the quilt, not realizing that it would take two years and over 2,000 pieces to complete the

project. Some of those 2,000 pieces were only ¼" in size, and a lot of the reverse appliqué involved even smaller shapes."

The quilt's top was made entirely from 100% cotton and silk fabrics and was all appliquéd. Asked if she would do anything differently if starting today, Joan replies, "I would have drawn my original pattern larger than 8½" x 11". The drawing had to be modified to a full-size quilt." Joan adds, "I probably would have also organized my pattern pieces better. Because the four corner designs are identical, it would have been easier to have kept each corner separated. I didn't do that so I had to put four 'puzzles' together. I also realized that an ⅛" to ¼" needle turn area looks good on paper but is quite difficult to do!"

Asked about the effects of completing this quilt and winning her award, Joan says, "Both were recognition that my skills are sound and of good quality and that my many years of paying attention to detail in my work were important." About the current

Asked what effect completing this quilt had on her life, Joan says, "It was important to me that I could finish a piece that at first seemed impossible to complete."

BIRDS
A-HUMMING,
IRIS
A-BLOOMING
61" x 81"
1990
Joan Rollins

heightened interest in quilting, Joan says, "Quilting is an art form that is finally being recognized; the people who quilt are interested in more than just financial gain."

Debra Wagner
Hutchinson, Minnesota

Ohio Bride's Quilt

Speaking of OHIO BRIDE'S QUILT, Debra Wagner says, "It was based on four antique quilts. Two were navy and white, and two were red and white. Although the sets and difficulty of the piecing varied, all of the quilts were variations on the Feathered Star pattern, and had the same distinct urn and flower quilting pattern."

Viewer's Choice

1990 AQS Show & Contest

100% cotton fabrics were used for this machine pieced and machine quilted quilt with trapunto. A cotton batt was also used, and polyester fill for the trapunto.

Debra comments on her initial response to the quilt, "I hated this quilt when I was finished with it. I had had nothing but trouble with it. I know I am not the only quilter who has had this experience. I was totally ignorant of the quilt's beauty; I saw only the hassle! Little did I know that after being away from it for a few months, I would view the quilt as one

of my favorites! Time has erased the bad memories. I don't even remember now what it was I had problems with. That experience taught me an important lesson: don't judge a quilt until you have put some distance between the creating and the finished product."

Debra, who holds a BS in Clothing, Textiles and Design from the University of Wisconsin/ Stout, has been quilting since 1987. She also spins and weaves, knits, crochets and does needlepoint. She makes lace, including bobbin lace, Battenburg lace

and lace net darning on bridal illusion. She also does embroideries, including cutwork, Hardanger, and drawn thread work.

She comments on her quilting, "Because I am slightly color blind, prints and muted or multicolor quilts tend to look like a gray/brown muddle to me. I see clearly only shapes and textures; subtle colors or illusions are lost on me. In my quilts, I prefer working with primary solid or near solid colors, with high contrast fabrics like white or ivory."

Debra says she was shocked at winning the Viewer's Choice award: "At the time of the contest I was still obsessed with the problems of construction. Winning made me take a second look!" She adds, "Winning an award is a great feeling. It validates your choice of color, and design. In addition, the cash prize helps to finance other projects."

About quiltmaking, Debra says, "The biggest single difference between quilting and other needlework is the network of people and corporations involved. My other

"I am drawn to the tactile facet of textiles, rather than color or print. In fact I prefer single color or white work in all forms of textiles."

OHIO BRIDE'S
QUILT
81" x 81"
1989
Debra Wagner

needlework is very singular; it is worked in private without many chances to exchange ideas with other artists or display work. For much of this needlework, supplies available are limited, or require ordering outside the United States. Quilting seems to have fostered a huge following that enjoys the fellowship as much as the actual work. As for supplies, there are so many different tools and fabrics available it is mind boggling and exciting! Everything is in wonderful excess!"

Dawn E. Amos
Rapid City, South Dakota

Looking Back II: Silent Cries

Asked what inspired LOOKING BACK II: SILENT CRIES, Dawn E. Amos replies, "The desire to deal with the culture of the Native American and try to incorporate 'real feeling' into a quilt."

Dawn continues, explaining that her "heart went into this quilt," the second in a series of works about the thoughts, emotions, and experiences of Native American people. She reveals that

Viewer's Choice

1990 AQS Show & Contest
Wall Quilt

each element of the design is meaningful, but adds that she is reluctant to fully discuss exactly why she selected each symbol or aspect. She explains, "I don't want to limit the viewer to my own vision."

Dawn used hand-dyed fabrics in this quilt, and the work is entirely appliquéd. She enjoys the subtle colors of hand-dyed fabric.

Dawn acknowledges the importance of her guild in her development as a quilter. "If you need to learn about how to do something, you can always find someone to teach you within the guild," she says.

A drawing class was also very influential in Dawn's life. Already a painter, she had thought that she was beyond Drawing I, but now acknowledges that the class proved to be helpful. Dawn has not painted since she began quilting 12 years ago, but still sketches. She some-

times wishes she had more training in color, but feels it is better to follow her own instincts.

Asked to comment on her response to winning this award, Dawn says, "Each individual has a vision. As a result, when you are dealing with the public, you are not going to please everybody." Dawn is delighted viewers have strongly responded to this particular quilt: "Receiving a Viewer's Choice award gives a person a great deal of satisfaction."

Dawn E. Amos and family

"Winning the Viewer's Choice award makes you feel that perhaps what you are doing is really okay."

LOOKING
BACK II:
SILENT CRIES
60" X 50"
1989
Dawn E. Amos

Quilt Show & Contest

1991

The seventh annual American Quilter's Society Quilt Show & Contest was held April 25 through 28, 1991, at the Executive Inn Riverfront in Paducah, Kentucky.

Judges for the show were Judy Mathieson, Woodland Hills, CA; Jeanette Muir, Morrestown, NJ; Judi Warren, Maumee, OH.

Workshops/Lectures/Seminars were sponsored by Pfaff American Sales Corporation, the Welcome Tea by Hancock Fabrics, and the Fashion Show by Hobbs Bonded Fibers and the American Quilter's Society.

Category award sponsors were as follows:

Best of Show, American Quilter's Society
Gingher Award for Workmanship, Gingher, Inc.
First Quilt Award, DreamSpinners
Traditional Pieced, Amateur, Hobbs Bonded Fibers
Traditional Pieced, Professional, Coats & Clark
Innovative Pieced, Amateur, Fairfield Processing Corp.

Innovative Pieced, Professional, Hoffman California Fabrics
Appliqué, Amateur, V.I.P. Fabrics
Appliqué, Professional, Mountain Mist
Other Techniques, Amateur/Professional, EZ International
Theme: Stars, Amateur/Professional, The Patchwork Place, Inc.
Group, Amateur/Professional, Swiss-Metrosene, Inc.
Best Wall Quilt, RJR Fashion Fabrics
Wall Quilt, Amateur, Silver Dollar City
Wall Quilt, Professional, Fiskars
Pictorial Wall Quilt, Amateur/Professional, Viking Sewing Machine Co.
Viewer's Choice, Quilt, Come Quilt with Me
Viewer's Choice, Wall Quilt, American Quilter's Society

In each category three awards were made: 1st place, $1000; 2nd place, $800; 3rd place, $500. The Gingher Award for Excellence of Workmanship was a $10,000 award; the Best of Show Award, $12,000; the Best Wall Quilt Award, $5,000; and the First Quilt Award, $500.

The exhibit included over 400 quilts, representing 48 states and Australia, Belgium, Canada, England, France, Finland, Germany, Japan, Republic of South Africa, and Switzerland. Viewers attending were asked to select their favorite quilts, and two Viewer's Choice Awards were made after the show.

The fifth quilted fashion contest sponsored by Hobbs Bonded Fibers was held, as was a non-competitive exhibit of quilted stars. Once again, the entire city of Paducah celebrated quilters and quiltmaking with special events, and over 30,000 people came to enjoy them.

The grand opening of the Museum of the American Quilter's Society added a most special event to the 1991 show. On April 25, during the show, this new 30,000 sq. ft. facility at 215 Jefferson St., in downtown Paducah, opened its doors, with three exciting exhibitions in place. During the show over 10,000 visited the museum. With the addition of MAQS, Paducah can now be called "Quilt City, U.S.A." all year long.

Nancy Ann Sobel
Brooktondale, New York

Dawn Splendor

Nancy Ann Sobel comments, "This quilt was probably the most challenging quilt I have ever made; at times I felt stretched beyond my ability and several times I almost abandoned the project." Nancy explains, "The inspiration came from our daughter Christi, who suggested that I do a series on the times of day. DAWN SPLENDOR is an entirely original quilt. All of the designs are my own, and were influenced by personal observations of my environment." Nancy adds, "I try to not be influenced by any other quilters or quilts; I try to follow my heart – I have never even taken a class."

best of show

1991 AQS Show & Contest

The quilt is made of 100% cottons and the techniques used include machine piecing, hand appliqué, embroidery, and quilting done with several hoop sizes. The quilting includes very close echo quilting and quilted designs of flowers, leaves, and birds.

Continuing to discuss the development of DAWN SPLENDOR, Nancy says, "It was hard to stick with the colors I observed at dawn; I had the feeling that they didn't go together right. I even felt a little silly about the spider and web in the center, but it seemed to need to be there."

Giving more insight into the design, Nancy says, "Victorian gingerbread, so abundant in New York state, has captured the artist in me, and so it also found its way into this quilt series." Asked

if she would do anything differently if beginning the quilt now, Nancy says, "My family and I agree that nothing should be changed about the quilt itself. However, I would keep better notes in my journal and work harder at setting goals."

"Completing this quilt," says Nancy, "was a victory, because the idea was new and challenging, and I wondered if I would really follow through with it." About her award she comments, "Being shy and preferring to maintain a very low profile, I felt a little uncomfortable being a sudden celebrity because of winning the award. However, the encouragement it provided spurs me on to finish this series regardless of how long it takes. It's nice to see that people beyond my family appreciate the work of my hands and heart."

Asked why she thinks quilting is so popular today, Nancy replies, "This is a hard question to answer without being quite philosophical. Each person has his or her own reason for being interested in quiltmaking. Thirty plus years ago, I quilted

"This quilt was originally intended to be a family heirloom, so it was made with lots of love and care."

DAWN
SPLENDOR
94" x 94"
©1990
Nancy Ann
Sobel

Museum of AQS Collection

because I loved it, regardless of my being teased. Back then, interest in quiltmaking was nearly extinct, and quilts were treated as being very ordinary household objects. I'm still trying to understand today's sudden popularity myself."

Julia Overton Needham
Knoxville, Tennessee

Tennessee Pink Marble

Speaking about the development of this award winning quilt, Julia Overton Needham says, "I had just finished a quilt – ANEMONES – which involved black and other dark colors and all straight lines. The next one had to involve light colors and curved lines." Julia continues, "Material purchased at a mill in North Carolina was the impetus for the quilt. The marbleized pink fabric matched a border fabric I already had."

gingher award

for workmanship
1991 AQS Show & Contest

About the construction of TENNESSEE PINK MARBLE, Julia says, "Cottons and cotton blends were used. The quilt was totally hand made with trapunto, and echo and stipple quilting." She adds, "The backing on the quilt was quite a departure for me. It, too, was a fabric I had bought at a mill. The colors in the top were duplicated in this other fabric, so I felt compelled to use them together."

Of her background Julia says, "I started a quilt when I was 13 and finished it in 1976. I'm a self-taught quilter who explores all of the printed material I can find." She adds, "I have never had any input from anyone – not even my husband. So if anything's wrong, it's my fault."

Asked if she would do anything differently if beginning the quilt now, Julia replies, "Yes, I would probably take more time to plan

the entire quilt before starting. I get in such a hurry to start the actual construction that I sometimes don't plan completely enough." She continues, "Numerous problems arose that necessitated some major adjustments. Before I had finished, I was sick of the quilt and had no hope for any ribbons. But I did send it to the Dollywood quilt show, and much to my surprise it won a Blue Ribbon and the Best Workmanship award in that show."

Julia was delighted to win a second workmanship award at the American Quilter's Society show. She comments, "I was so pleased that the quilt had been juried into the show that I couldn't believe it when it was declared the Gingher Workmanship Award winner. I still have trouble believing it."

Asked why quilting is enjoying such widespread popularity now, Julia suggests it is "because we have so many great organizations, guilds, books, magazines, museums and quilt shows that promote the art."

"They say lightning doesn't strike twice, but it does. It struck first in 1988 when my LAVENDER BLUE won the Gingher Workmanship Award!"

TENNESSEE
PINK MARBLE
72" x 88"
1990
Julia Overton
Needham

Museum of AQS Collection

Irma Gail Hatcher
Conway, Arkansas

Ozark Oaks

Quilter Irma Gail Hatcher explains that the design for OZARK OAKS was developed on graph paper, the same way she designs all of her quilts. Working with graph paper first allows her to "easily manipulate the blocks to get different effects." Irma Gail adds, "This particular design was influenced by an antique tree quilt I saw on a *Lady's Circle Patchwork Quilts* magazine cover."

first place

1991 AQS Show & Contest Traditional Pieced, Ama

The quilt is made of 100% cotton fabric, with a cotton batting. To construct the quilt, Irma Gail used fast-pieced triangles, traditional piecing, appliqué, stipple quilting in her own original design, and crosshatch quilting. Irma Gail adds, "The white border alone took me four months to stipple quilt!"

Asked if she would do anything differently if starting this quilt now, Irma Gail says, "No. I really like this quilt. The only thing I was afraid of was that no one else would like it. But fortunately that has not been the case." OZARK OAKS has, in fact, won several awards with cash prizes and has also appeared in a number of publications, including *Quilter's Newsletter Magazine's* "Peerless Patchwork."

About her background, Irma Gail says, "While living in Michigan I began quilting, to learn another craft. A year later we moved to Arkansas and I became involved with the Arkansas Quilter's Guild. The very friendly people there inspired me to really try quilting and to even create my own designs." Irma Gail adds, "I've been really hooked for 10 years now, and plan to continue for many more years because I already have on hand enough fabrics to last until I'm at least 92."

Irma Gail continues, "I have been involved in quite a few other crafts: stained glass, cross-stitch, wood carving, Hardanger, corn-shuck dolls, handmade dolls, etc. But these crafts were all learned by reading books and were done alone. The support one gets by being in a local quilt guild makes a great deal of difference. I now have many people with whom to share my love of quilting. My quilting friends are my best friends."

"I have been involved in quite a few other crafts, but it is quilting that has finally put all of my artistic talents to work!"

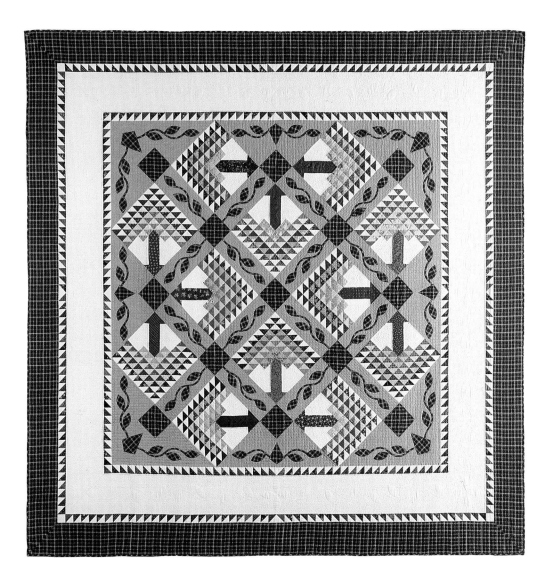

OZARK OAKS
92" x 92"
1990
Irma Gail
Hatcher

Joyce Stewart
Rexburg, Idaho

Nihon No Onna No Ko

Joyce Stewart explains, "The design for the block was from a pattern by Amy Myoraku. My son had been in Japan for two years, and I had bought a lot of Japanese wood block printed material." She adds, "Dressing each Japanese girl was great fun. The main color scheme was blue and rust but I managed to include everything else, too – there are at least 200 different fabrics in the quilt."

second place

1991 AQS Show & Contest Traditional Pieced, Ama

Speaking about her background in quilting, Joyce says, "In 1982 I was asked to make a quilt top for my church group. Everyone was to quilt on it, and it would then be sold at an auction. I had never seen 'real quilts' before and most people were making cheater cloth quilts or doing whole-cloth quilting on tricot. I didn't want to do either, so I found a book with a few quilted blocks in it."

She continues, "I made a Rolling Star pattern for the quilt and put a border on it. It brought in the most money at the auction, but I thought it was a lot of work and didn't do anything else with quilting for about a year. Then I signed up for a class on strip-pieced star quilts. After that, I made strip-pieced quilts for about a year and then, using Jinny Beyer's book, I made a sampler quilt. Next, I found out about quilt magazines and quilt shows and I really got hooked."

Speaking more about this quilt, Joyce says, "I worked on it off and on for about four years. I really loved it, but I kept having to do a wedding quilt or baby quilt, or there would be a contest I wanted to enter – this quilt took longer than any other one to finish."

About her techniques, Joyce says, "I soak all of my fabrics when I buy them, to get all of the loose color out so I won't have any problems later. However, after this quilt was all done there were four places on the back where the color had come through from the front. So I appliquéd a Japanese girl and three different Japanese lanterns in strategic positions."

Commenting on quiltmaking, Joyce says, "I know a lot of people who can make a quilt once in a while for a new baby or for a couple getting married, and then not make another one for a year or two. I have to always be making a quilt – I don't care if I have a use for it or not. I just want to be creating a quilt – trying out different color combinations – making up new patterns – seeing the effects of putting this print with that print – seeing how the quilting enhances everything I have done."

"I always sewed my own clothes, and did other crafts and needlework such as cross-stitch, but I could always take them or leave them. Quilting, though, is a must!"

NIHON NO
ONNA NO KO
80" x 100"
1991
Joyce Stewart

Patricia Mahoney
Santa Maria, California

Reflections

Asked about the development of this quilt, Patricia Mahoney explains, "Seven or eight of the squares were begun in a Roberta Horton workshop and then put away and forgotten for a year or two." Patricia continues,

third place

1991 AQS Show & Contest Traditional Pieced, Ama

"When my husband was hospitalized I found the squares again, put them together, and started making more. The quilt became a portable project that could be taken back and forth, to and from the hospital."

Patricia adds, "Working on this quilt during my husband's long terminal illness was a comforting and satisfying activity. REFLECTIONS will always have a very special meaning for me."

About her background, Patricia says, "I began quilting about 25 years ago. I was always looking for something extra in my life, and when I discovered quiltmaking, I was hooked right from the beginning. I try to give my best effort to every quilt I make, and I find the work a constant source of pleasure – when the quilt is finished, that is – I seem to struggle a lot while a quilt is being made!"

Asked if there is anything special she would like people to know about this quilt, Patricia replies, "No. It seems ironic to me that this quilt has been successful. There was no plan involved – it just happened, square by square. The quilts I make usually start with a sketch or an idea and then go on. Their development is more planned. Maybe there is a message here – for me to be freer."

Patricia says this of her award: "Winning this award has made a difference to me. First of all, it was fun to win, and it also made me feel that in a certain sense my work is valuable. Working on quilts and spending a lot of time sewing is time-consuming. Sometimes I am not sure whether what I enjoy doing is worthwhile or not."

Patricia adds, "Being involved in quiltmaking is very important to me. I find fulfillment in making quilts. Other arts and crafts don't have the appeal and satisfaction for me."

"There were no special materials or techniques used for this quilt – just ordinary cotton fabric and an Ohio Star pattern."

REFLECTIONS
90" x 103"
1990
Patricia
Mahoney

Debra Wagner
Hutchinson, Minnesota

Rail Through The Rockies

Debra Wagner explains, "This variation of the traditional New York Beauty pattern is adapted from three antique quilts, all from the second half of the nineteenth century. In one quilt I loved the double arcs; in another the tiny pieces, the detailed quilting and the trapunto; in the third, the diagonal set." The quilt is machine pieced of 100% cotton fabrics and machine quilted, with trapunto added.

first place

1991 AQS Show & Contest Traditional Pieced, Pro

Speaking of her background, Debra says, "I've only been quilting for about five years, but have had a lifelong obsession with antique textiles, including quilts. My obsession goes beyond wanting to own or understand antiques; I want to know what it is like to create the textile." She gives an example, "I would guess that I am the only person in the country who received a working copy of an antique spinning wheel for my high school graduation gift!"

Debra continues, "Quilting was a natural step in my growing repertoire of textile techniques. Because of my background (a B.S. in clothing, textiles and design from the University of Wisconsin-Stout), I am well versed in hand stitching and embroidery, but I prefer to use the sewing machine. I've done machine embroidery since I was ten years old, so the sewing machine is like an extension of my hands. The machine makes it possible for me to quilt very quickly

and accurately."

Of this award-winning quilt, Debra says, "I made this quilt for myself. I usually choose a pattern because it is difficult and a challenge or because someone else wants a particular design. I had wanted to make this quilt for a long time; I am crazy about curved triangle designs." Debra adds, "Because of the sheer volume of pieces, I developed a method of piecing I call 'striplate.' It reduces the actual number of individual pieces by one half or more. I also learned about being extremely accurate and I became familiar with where I could cheat, and where I could not."

On the subject of the current popularity of quilting, Debra says, "I think part of the appeal of quiltmaking is its extremes. On one end is the basic bed quilt – so simple it requires almost no sewing experience and can be completed in a day or two. On the other end are the intricate quilts that are art, not household linens. Few textile arts offer as many skill levels or avenues for self-expression."

"Of all the awards I have won for my quilts, this one was the most special because this quilt was one I had made for myself."

RAIL THROUGH
THE ROCKIES
70" x 92"
1990
Debra Wagner

Judy Sogn
Seattle, Washington

Starburst

Judy Sogn explains, "STARBURST is a variation of my quilt FOREVER GREEN, which was inspired by Margit Echols' block called Stars and Pines." Further discussing the quilt's development, Judy says, "STARBURST was a true joy to work on, and I find it remains my favorite quilt so far."

second place

1991 AQS Show & Contest Traditional Pieced, Pro

Judy continues, "I enjoy taking inspiration from quilts that I see in books and magazines and then changing things here and there to make the quilt my own. I drafted an original Feathered Star variation and then used a set from Judy Martin's book on Lone Stars." Judy adds, "I also enjoy working with the optical illusion of a third dimension and I used that effect for the border."

The quilt is machine pieced and hand quilted.

Judy also explains that though most of the fabrics were commercially printed or dyed, there are two light turquoise prints that she over-dyed with fiber-reactive dye herself, to achieve the value that she wanted.

Asked if she would do anything differently if beginning the quilt today, Judy says, "I can't think of anything that I would change if I were to remake STARBURST, except perhaps to put a print fabric on the back or even piece the back instead of using the solid blue fabric that I did."

About her background, Judy says, "I started quilting in 1982 after having sewn clothing for many years, and having also knitted and done many needlepoint pillows and pictures. I wanted to make Christmas gifts for relatives and many craft-type patterns were available at that time. I made several projects that involved a variety of miscellaneous quilt-related techniques. I found that I enjoyed each project and finally I decided to make a sampler for my mother- and father-in-law for Christmas." Judy says she has been quilting ever since.

Commenting on the popularity of quilting, Judy says, "Quiltmaking is definitely different from any other needlework that I have tried. I know of no other type of stitchery that has such an extensive industry devoted to it." She adds, "The fellowship of other quilters and quilt groups adds to the appeal of quiltmaking for me."

"In 1982 I decided to make a sampler for my mother- and father-in-law for Christmas. Before long I was hopelessly hooked."

STARBURST
95" x 95"
1990
Judy Sogn

Betty Ekern Suiter
Racine, Wisconsin

Lilies Of The Field

"A photo of a circa 1850 quilt made in New England was the inspiration for LILIES OF THE FIELD," says Betty Ekern Suiter. She explains, "I changed some elements of the antique quilt to come up with the new design for my own quilt."

The fabrics in this quilt are all 100% cotton: etched muslin, blue/mauve print and soldier blue solid. The fern spray quilting pattern is done in trapunto and a ¼" grid is quilted throughout on the background.

third place

1991 AQS Show & Contest Traditional Pieced, Pro

Speaking of the development of the quilt, Betty says, "I had always wanted to do a lily pattern but was looking for a difficult design. I found one in that 1850's quilt!" Continuing, Betty says, "I enjoy doing trapunto and like the effects it creates." She adds, "The ¼" grid quilting was the finishing touch." The quilt is all hand quilted and took Betty two years to complete.

Asked if she would do anything differently if beginning the quilt today, Betty replies, "No, as of this date it is my favorite piece. It is my husband's favorite as well."

Betty says of her background, "I began quilting in

1979, with some old quilt blocks that had been my grandmother's, and I quite instantly got hooked." Betty continues, "I had worked for seven years as a draftsman which was good background for drafting quilt patterns." She adds that she is a National Quilting Association Master Quilter.

About her award Betty says, "It is always a thrill to win in Paducah. This is my second award from AQS. It adds fuel to the fire that keeps me striving for perfection in my quiltmaking."

In response to our question about why quilting is enjoying such popularity, Betty says, "It takes complete dedication to complete a quilt and gives one a feeling of accomplishment to succeed. Many crafts are just a fad of the time. Quilting has survived through the ages." She adds, "Quilts can be made to beautify a home or just to keep warm, a consideration to remember in Wisconsin."

"LILIES OF THE FIELD contains 3,697 pieces. Each pieced block has 111 pieces, and the Flying Geese border 967 pieces."

LILIES OF
THE FIELD
77" x 105"
1990
Betty Ekern
Suiter

Chizuko (Hana) Hill
Cadiz, Kentucky

Autumn Nostalgia

Speaking of the inspiration for this quilt, Chizuko Hana Hill explains, "One year I became rather nostalgic when autumn leaves started falling. I was thinking about my daughter in Japan, wishing we were together under the falling leaves. So the big origami bird is me, and the small one is my daughter."

first place

1991 AQS Show & Contest Innovative Pieced, Ama

Chizuko says this quilt's design is "semi-original." She explains: "I used a leaf pattern I found in the August 1986 issue of the magazine *McCall's Needlework & Crafts.* It is the block Nancy Halpern designed for her quilt TO CAPTURE THE FALL, which appeared in a photo on page 77 of that issue. In making my quilt, I used the pattern in the magazine, but I arranged the leaves differently and also used purple and lavender colors instead of the fall colors Nancy Halpern used in her quilt."

Chizuko continues, "The origami bird block is one I found a pattern for in an issue of the Japanese magazine *Patchwork Quilt Tsushin.* I am also especially attached to the origami bird – my Japanese name 'Chizuko' means 'a thousand cranes.' My parents gave me this name, praying for a long life. The Japanese proverb 'tsuru wa sennen' means cranes live a thousand years. Therefore, a thousand cranes would live forever – 1,000 X 1,000 years." Chizuko adds, "The way the leaves and birds are arranged is very similar to Japanese kimono designs."

This quilt is made of cot-

tons. The leaves were hand pieced, and the origami bird and fence were appliquéd.

Asked about her background, Chizuko says, "A friend of mine asked me to take a lap quilting class with her in April 1985. I was fortunate to see the first annual AQS Show during the time I was taking lessons. I was deeply impressed with the many beautiful quilts. I had had no prior knowledge of quilting whatsoever."

Chizuko adds, "I am currently addicted to quilting. I have entered many other quilts into AQS Quilt Shows and other national competitions and had some selected as finalists." She adds, "While I try to create some original designs, I also like to make traditional quilts."

Asked if there is anything different she would do if beginning this quilt today, Chizuko replies, "Surprisingly I had no trouble in putting this quilt together and I am satisfied with it." She adds that its award has been very meaningful for her: "It has fulfilled my desires and given me recognition as a quilter."

"To complete a quilt is a big challenge. You need patience and perseverance. When I complete a quilt I feel a great self-satisfaction which other crafts do not instill in me."

AUTUMN
NOSTALGIA
67" x 90"
1990
Chizuko (Hana)
Hill

Adrien Rothschild
Baltimore, Maryland

Desert Blooms

Adrien Rothschild says this original design was actually derived from doodling. She was doodling and there suddenly appeared foliage that suggested a cactus. Adrien relates this quilt to her life and work: "I like working with earth tones –

second place

1991 AQS Show & Contest Innovative Pieced, Ama

colors that remind one about the desert – and I have a large collection of cacti. In fact, about all of the plants in my house are cacti. For some reason I like them. Perhaps this is also by default. I leave Maryland every winter to seek the sun, and my house-sitters have a tendency to let everything die – everything but the cacti, which survive. Maybe they are just all that are left."

This exploration of color is constructed in commercial cottons and is machine-pieced and hand-quilted. Adrien is completely self-taught as a quiltmaker. She explains, "Until I started to quilt, about all the sewing I had done was that required to replace a button or take up the cuffs in my pants. I started my first quilt in 1978, not knowing the first thing about what I was doing. As a result, most of my early quilts fell apart. No one in my family quilted, and I never even bothered to buy a book on quilting until 1985."

The first quilt Adrien made was a copy of a painting she had done. "I was a painter and photographer and had done much painting. My mother is an artist and I just seemed to soak it in. I wanted a quilt for my bed and I knew I didn't just want to copy someone else's design. I especially liked one of my hard-edge paintings with geometric shapes, so I decided to use it as my design. I did change the col-

ors because of the limited fabrics that were available. Color gradations weren't available at that time. I'm still not sure why I made a quilt. Maybe something inside me knew that my design sense was more appropriate for quilts than for anything else."

To date Adrien has made forty to fifty quilts. Aside from a very early appliqué landscape quilt that Adrien calls "somewhat an aberration" (though it remains a favorite), DESERT BLOOMS was the first of her quilts that was representational. She adds, "Most of my quilts since then have been representational. I'm not really certain why. Maybe just playing around with straight lines and abstract blocks finally became boring."

Asked if there is anything she would change about the quilt if beginning it now, Adrien says, "No. I am very pleased with the effect – I think I may do more flowers."

"Before quilting I was a painter and photographer. From the beginning my paintings were hard-edge geometrics – clearly I was destined to be a quiltmaker."

DESERT
BLOOMS
88" x 88"
©1989
Adrien
Rothschild

Janet Robinson
Highlands Ranch, Colorado

Color Rhythms

Janet Robinson began the design for this machine pieced and hand quilted quilt in a class taught by Nancy Crow. Janet explains, "The black and white study I produced in Nancy's class can be seen on the back of the quilt. After the class I put the design aside for about six months, then redesigned and pieced the front of the quilt."

third place

*1991 AQS Show & Contest
Innovative Pieced, Ama*

Continuing to discuss the development of the quilt, Janet says, "Because my next love, second to quiltmaking, is music – I play violin with a community symphony – I wanted to make a quilt in which the colors reflected some aspect of music. As I was choosing colors for my repeat block, I wanted them to change with each row, yet retain the same essential

flow of design. Even though the colors move and change, the basic design of the quilt, the basic rhythm, remains the same and becomes the most important element. The colors, as they move across and down the quilt, enhance this rhythm and give it life."

Discussing her background, Janet says, "I began quilting in 1985, in order to use up a lot of scraps of fabric I had accumulated from

sewing clothes. I took a three-day workshop with Diane Logan and joined a neighborhood quilting bee. My first two quilts were made from fabric scraps and were for my two children. By that time I knew I wanted to design my own quilts rather than reproduce traditional quilt designs." She adds, "I have been working toward that goal ever since."

Asked about the effect of her award, Janet says, "When I finished this quilt, I felt that I had achieved my goal of several years – my goal to successfully design my own quilts and move beyond traditional designs to a more individual artistic approach to quilting." She adds, "Winning the award gave me the stimulus to continue designing and producing art quilts. This quilt will appear in the Quilt San Diego show, 'Visions – The Art of the Quilt,' and will travel from 1992 to 1994 with other pieces from the show."

"I think quilting appeals to me and to others because of the support quilters receive from other quilters."

COLOR
RHYTHMS
68" x 80"
©1991
Janet Robinson

Eileen Bahring Sullivan
Columbia, South Carolina

Peace Lily

Discussing the origins of PEACE LILY, Eileen Bahring Sullivan says, "I was asked to design a small quilt using the sew & flip technique, to be included in a book on foundation-pieced projects. The Spathiphyllum plant, well known to us by its generic name of Peace Lily or White Flag, is very linear and angular in its structure, so I chose it for the quilt." Eileen adds, "This small quilt proved so satisfying that I knew I had to explore the possibilities even further, and thus began the creation of PEACE LILY."

first place

1991 AQS Show & Contest
Innovative Pieced, Pro

Eileen continues, "The sew & flip technique made the piecing of very sharp angles, the multiple fabric changes, and the integrated borders quite feasible. The fabrics were all commercially dyed or printed; most were solid cottons, with a few drapery chintz fabrics." Eileen adds, "This was the second quilt based on floral motifs and utilizing the foundation pieced technique."

Speaking of the quiltmaking process, Eileen says, "While it was begun simply as an artistic expression, this quilt took on its own life and meaning because of the time during which it was created. While I was working on it, I and the rest of the world had a constant eye and ear on CNN, following the events of Desert Shield, and later, Desert Storm." Eileen continues, "A correlation was eventually made between current events and the subject of my quilt through an image on the back and a message quilted into the border. The back of the quilt contains a small patchwork globe from which light radiates, and the words 'May this lily of peace stand as a symbol to our world' flow through the border."

Eileen notes, "Resolution for both the quilt and Desert Storm occurred simultaneously. The final stitches were sewn as the War in the Gulf ended! Maybe the words in the border will be heeded."

About her award, Eileen says, "1991 was the second year for me in the same category – to be able to repeat the win of 1990 was extremely exciting. I think it shows that it is worth striving for work that reaches beyond traditional images yet retains the technical integrity we have come to value as quiltmakers."

On quiltmaking, Eileen says, "Even the most traditional interpretation of a published pattern requires its maker to become part of the work, adding her 'personal stamp' through the decisions she makes."

Photo: Renee Ittner-McManus/The State, Columbia, SC.

"Quiltmaking and the decisions it requires from the maker offer great potential for personalizing the work, even if only through the challenge of fabric selection."

PEACE LILY
67" x 82"
©1991
Eileen Bahring
Sullivan

Moneca Calvert
Rocklin, California

Spring's Promise

"SPRING'S PROMISE," says Moneca Calvert, "is #17 in my ongoing series of Contemporary Pieced and Placed Clamshell quilts." Moneca continues, "The two black background, flower patterned fabrics used were the inspiration for the title. The black and white outline blossoms with no color suggested flowers just waiting to burst into color." She adds,

second place

1991 AQS Show & Contest Innovative Pieced, Pro

"The fabric also inspired the overall design created by the various twelve-inch pieced Clamshells set in mirror image." Constructed of cotton fabrics, the quilt is machine pieced, and machine and hand quilted. The center black section is very heavily quilted by machine with a gold thread.

Asked about her work, Moneca says, "I had no idea of the endless design exploration this three-sided 'block' would present. To my knowledge, single Clamshells had

never been used as individual blocks and set in mirror image to create vertical and horizontal rows that run clear out to the edges of a quilt. Nor had the design appeared large enough that further design elements could be added within each Clamshell." Moneca comments, "I plan to continue to work in this Clamshell series because the design possibilities are endless." She adds, "The very unusual three-sided nature of this block actually does the designing itself!"

About awards and compe-

titions, Moneca says, "I enjoy the competition and I find awards very meaningful." She explains that it was by making award-winning quilts that she was able to quite quickly "carve a career" for herself in quiltmaking. She began teaching within three years of beginning quilting, and within four years had won the grand prize at the 1986 Great American Quilt Festival, which brought international recognition. Moneca's one comment about current judging for awards is, "I think it is the merit of the work that should be judged, rather than the maker's background." She adds, "It is sometimes difficult to ignore the maker's history, but as much as possible we need to just consider the work."

As a quiltmaker Moneca is largely self-taught. There were no quilts in her "formative years." She comments, "I didn't know quilts were still being made until I was 20 years old, but I do have over 40 years of sewing experience." Moneca discovered the current quilting world in 1982. She comments, "My first class was with Katie

"I found the quilting world ten years ago and knew immediately that this was a 'career' I wanted to cultivate for the rest of my life!"

SPRING'S
PROMISE
95" x 95"
©1991
Moneca Calvert

Pasquini and happened quite by chance. That led to the further discovery of related events such as shows, guilds, conferences, and quilt publications – and the knowledge that I, too, could be a part of all this activity." With national awards and the resulting coverage of her work in national quilting publications, Moneca has been teaching on a national level since 1985.

Asked to comment on the current popularity of quilt-making, Moneca says, "American patchwork is truly an art born in this country, and everyone can relate to the tactile nature of quilts. It is our American heritage, regardless of our origins before America."

Mary Morgan
Little Rock, Arkansas

Spinoff

Asked to talk about the development of this quilt, Mary Morgan says, "SPINOFF was the third quilt I made using a simple, three-piece block pattern which consists of one large and two small triangles." She adds, "Many different effects can be achieved through various changes in color and direction."

third place

1991 AQS Show & Contest Innovative Pieced, Pro

Mary explains that all of the fabrics in the quilt are cottons, and all have been specially hand-dyed by her for the construction of this quilt. She adds, "The striped fabric was over-dyed. It was originally a commercially printed black and white striped fabric. I just over-dyed the stripe with a color." The quilt was machine pieced and hand quilted.

Speaking of her background, Mary says, "When I began quilting 20 years ago, suitable cotton fabrics were difficult to find and precious, and there were very limited numbers of quilting books available. In the area where I was living, quilt guilds and quilt classes were virtually unheard of." She adds, "For years I felt I as if I were the only quilter within 100 miles doing anything innovative."

Making quilts provides an important creative outlet for Mary. She finds she enjoys working with a simple pattern like the Pinwheel block to discover what possibilities it presents. In this particular quilt she achieved a spinning effect through the use of color and pattern, and is delighted that when people view the quilt they can see several different pinwheel patterns – small yellow ones, then a larger size with grays, and others for which the view must search. Mary comments, "I like to keep the pattern simple and rely on color changes for interest and excitement."

"I enjoy my quilt guild. It's fun being around people who share the same interest and who appreciate what I do."

SPINOFF
77" x 82"
1990
Mary Morgan

Jonathan Shannon
Belvedere Tiburon, California

July

Quilter Jonathan Shannon explains, "JULY was inspired by my love of sunflowers and summer days. The imagery first came to me in a dream." Further describing the development of this quilt, he elaborates: "In each of my quilts I set for myself the challenge of greater complexity in design and technique."

first place

1991 AQS Show & Contest
Appliqué, Amateur

Jonathan continues, "I am very interested in creating an emotional mood using space and light. In JULY I wanted the illusion of summer as it might appear in the mind's eye, not a realistic rendering of an actual scene. I like the kind of space that appears in dreams, where things are both different from reality and very believable."

Asked if he would do anything differently if beginning the quilt today, Jonathan replies, "I'm sure I would do everything differently today. Dreams constantly change."

Speaking of his back-ground, Jonathan says, "By early 1988, my business had become successful enough to allow me some free time to pursue other interests. I had worked with textiles both as a fashion and an interior designer during my diverse career, so fabric was not a mystery to me. Inspired by a photograph I decided to make a quilt."

He continues, "On my first trip to the fabric store I discovered *Quilter's Newsletter Magazine* and the compelling world of quiltmaking. While I am still co-owner of a bed-and-breakfast inn in San Francisco, I devote every bit of free time I have to the art of quiltmaking. In 1991, I became a National Quilting Association Certified Judge."

About awards, Jonathan says, "Discovering that I can make quilts that are appreciated by others has been an important milestone in my life. There were moments in the midst of the hundreds of hours of work I put into this quilt when I thought, 'What on earth am I doing this for? Real life is going by the door.' Seeing JULY hanging amongst so many exciting quilts at the AQS Show was validation for all the time spent, convincing me that this, too, is 'real life.' "

Asked about the popular-

"Textiles touch some magic chord in our souls. Their creation fills a spiritual need much deeper than the need for warmth or covering."

JULY
91" x 103"
©1991
Jonathan
Shannon

ity of quiltmaking, Jonathan comments, "Throughout history, ornamenting cloth has been a revered practice, used to communicate emotional imagery more than intellectual ideas. This level of communication unites people from diverse backgrounds and cultural experiences. Through quilts we share our 'humanness.'"

Mary Johnson
Munster, Indiana

Marys' Garden

Mary Johnson comments, "When my daughter Linn decided to draw an original quilt design for me to make, she had in mind a garden quilt that would recall the garden she had grown up with. Every plant and critter pictured flourished in our garden." Mary continues, "For Linn, it was important that each individual plant block

second place

1991 AQS Show & Contest
Appliqué, Amateur

or border be a complete representation and design in its own right, and that the elements also work together as a whole-cloth quilt – a bit chaotic and a bit overwhelming, like the garden itself."

About the techniques she used, Mary says, "I now exclusively use the needle-turn appliqué technique I learned from Nancy Pearson in 1983. The embroidery technique was developed by the Deerfield Society of Blue and White Needlework in around 1900. I saw beautiful examples of this work in the

Deerfield Museum, and I learned the technique from a book purchased there."

Mary speaks of her own background, "I made my first quilt in the 1940's after attending the Lake County Fair in Crown Point, Indiana. My husband, Earl, made my first patterns and templates. I made several quilts at that time, then went on to other things, and returned to quilting in the 1970's." She adds, "I've done handwork since kindergarten. It was a skill taught in the Austrian elementary school I attended. I have knitted, crocheted, and done embroidery, crewel

work, drawn work, cutwork, tatting, and appliqué."

Of this quilt, Mary says: "This quilt is very, very special to me. I still have a garden and we still share in the planting and harvesting, if not the weeding. The quilt itself is the reward of a unique creative collaboration between my daughter and me." Mary adds, "The drawings were black and white. Linn was very excited to see blocks come alive with fabrics and embroidery." Mary adds, "After winning in Paducah, I added a few more critters and doubled the amount of quilting so that the scale of the quilting would be in keeping with the scale of the appliquéd designs."

This quilt has brought Mary great joy. She comments, "When Linn and I get together and sometimes even when I'm alone, I open MARYS' GARDEN on the floor, and simply enjoy looking at it. I'm still overwhelmed that I actually created such a work. It seems to have a life and beauty of its own."

About the popularity of quilting, Mary says, "Quilt-making is truly a democratic

"I found much more variety of color and shade in the real garden than I ever imagined. Making this quilt has opened my eyes even more to the beauty of my everyday environment."

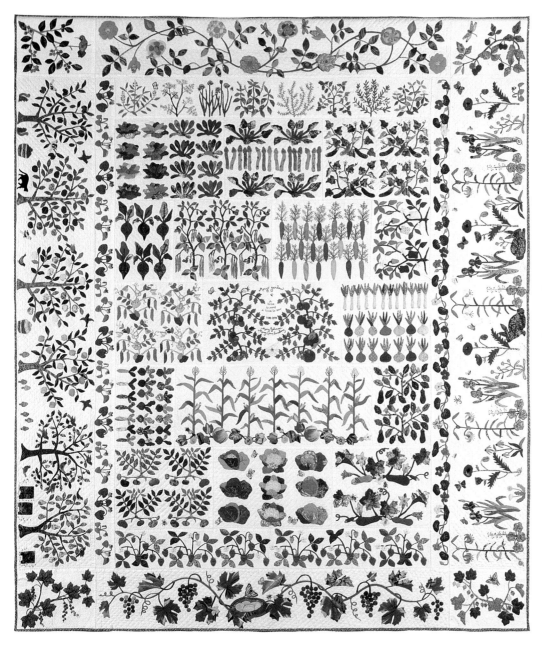

MARYS'
GARDEN
76" x 88"
©1991
Mary Johnson

art form. Anyone can be creative and successful, from a small child on. There is always something new to attempt, something new to express." She then adds, "The making of every quilt also has an individual story. Many times the making of the quilt became a life – or at least sanity – saver in the life of the quilter."

Patricia L. Styring
St. Augustine, Florida

Baltimore Album Nouveau With Angels

"BALTIMORE ALBUM NOUVEAU WITH ANGELS," says Patricia L. Styring, "was inspired by a number of older quilts." She explains, "Current books were used as references, but most influential were my friend Ira Inman's photographs of some of the original quilts in Baltimore. I had 8 X 10 copies made for myself."

third place

1991 AQS Show & Contest Appliqué, Amateur

Patricia says that over 60 different fabrics were used in the quilt. She explains that a number of techniques were incorporated as well: "I used appliqué, reverse appliqué, embroidery, and inking." She adds, "I used freezer paper on the back of every piece except for the flowing vines. To create a block I made every element ahead of time, then arranged the pieces on the background until I achieved the desired effect. Then I glued it all in place, stitched it, rinsed out the glue, and removed the paper

by cutting away the back."

Asked about the design, Patricia says, "The angels are original, as are the fuchsias. The house is my drawing of my house, made without even a photo for reference. As a result, there are a few errors! For example, I forgot the garage. (To me it is more important to be original than to be totally accurate.)" She continues, "The tree block has family names written on the berries. I like the flowing border with angels tying bows because it gives the impression of being orderly,

yet on closer inspection not all elements repeat. Some shapes, like the strawberries, appear only once – they were definitely too hard for me to include them on all four borders. In addition, the top corners differ from the bottom corners. The border satisfies a desire in me for asymmetry, even though it is part of a quilt that is the epitome of a traditional quilt."

Patricia began quilting seven years ago, when she was "tired of making clothing and wanted a more creative outlet." She adds, "My quilts now number 35, and each is signed, dated, and recorded in a log and photo book."

Asked if she would do anything differently if beginning this quilt today, Patricia says, "Perhaps be sure of the yardage required, so I would not end up having to piece together one border." She adds, "I had to design the vines to cover the seam, which is very curvy. The vines were so successful that no one has found the seam yet. Otherwise, I am very happy with the outcome."

About the effect of winning her award, Patricia says,

"It is hard to describe the effect of winning the AQS award without sounding almost silly. I know I will be happy even if I never win another contest!"

BALTIMORE ALBUM NOUVEAU WITH ANGELS
85" x 85"
1991
Patricia L. Styring

"My feet did not touch ground for a month at the thrill of being included with that stellar band of quilters who have won at AQS. Then, after the show, I was unsure of what to quilt next; the ideas stopped flowing for months. Now I again have ideas but am recovering from arm surgery for nerve damage, partly resulting from quilting this quilt."

Speaking about the strength of current interest in quilting, Patricia says, "For me, it is the originality of the medium that is attractive. I find that anything I can draw can be put onto fabric. The permanence of quilts is also attractive. The quilts remain when we are gone – how seductive, immortality!"

Dixie McBride
Eureka, California

Peacocks

Describing the inspiration for this quilt, Dixie McBride says, "I fell in love with a friend's Lone Star quilt with appliqué and wanted to make one just like it. Not satisfied with the results of numerous sketches and the completed star portion of my quilt, I put the project away in a dark closet for several years."

first place

1991 AQS Show & Contest
Appliqué, Pro

Then Dixie returned to the quilt: "After turning to my own pattern for a block with a peacock in it, I suddenly knew how I wanted to complete my Lone Star quilt. Ideas seemed to fill my head continuously, and I found I couldn't draw fast enough." Dixie adds, "Although the finished quilt is nothing like my friend's quilt, she is very proud of the way PEACOCKS turned out."

The fabrics in this quilt are all 100% cottons, and many different appliqué techniques were used in its creation, the main ones being finger turning and needle manipulation.

Dixie began quilting in 1979, after moving to Eureka, California. This community has many Victorian homes, and Dixie was also feeling the influence of living in one of the city's turn-of-the-century buildings. She comments, "It just seemed natural to make a quilt – just one." Dixie adds, "I took a class in adult educa-

tion and have quilted non-stop ever since that time."

Commenting on the making of PEACOCKS, Dixie says, "Development of this quilt was an awakening to me, in that it was the first time I had ever really let go of self imposed 'rules' and discovered the joys of designing my own work. The real freedom came after overhearing someone refer to me as a folk artist, and then explain what that meant in terms of creativity. One of the classes I now teach is a workshop on Folk Art Medallion Appliqué; I encourage all my students to discover their own hidden talents."

Asked about the effect of her award, Dixie says, "Winning the first place award in in the Professional Appliqué category at the American Quilter's Society Show was a big boost in my teaching and lecturing career. The exposure has been an invaluable aid to broadening my geographic horizons – I am now teaching, lecturing, and traveling across the country."

128

*"When a quilt is finished, I prefer to enjoy it just as it is.
All new ideas and growth in my quiltmaking go into the next quilts."*

PEACOCKS
83" x 83"
©1990
Dixie McBride

Rebekka Seigel
Owenton, Kentucky

Pre-pubescent Pool Party

Rebekka Seigel explains, "The inspiration for this piece was a photograph taken at a birthday party given for quiltmaker Sharee Roberts' daughter, Danielle. I spent a month living in Danielle's bedroom when I was serving as an artist-in-residence in a school in Ballard County, Kentucky."

second place

1991 AQS Show & Contest
Appliqué, Pro

Rebekka continues, "The photo was on her bulletin board and I was intrigued by what you could tell about each girl from the way she stood in the picture. I also liked the idea of portraying young girls at the time in their lives when they are just starting to bud into women. The metamorphosis is beginning and their bodies are transforming."

PRE-PUBESCENT POOL PARTY is constructed of cottons and poly/cottons, and was made using appliqué, reverse appliqué, machine piecing, embroidery, and hand quilting techniques.

Rebekka says of the quilt's development, "This quilt gave me the opportunity to continue to develop my use of appliqué to depict the human face and figure. I feel that with each face I attempt, I get a little closer to perfecting the technique."

Asked about the effect of her AQS award, Rebekka says, "As with any award I have won, this one helps validate the decision I made many years ago to see myself as an artist and to produce the best art I was capable of. This quilt is a major piece in the body of my work and it is one that nearly everyone who sees it can identify with." She adds, "Everyone has either gone through this transformation herself or had a sister, a cousin, or a friend who did. The imagery in this quilt freezes that moment of 'budding' for all time and reminds us once again how beautiful we are and how time changes us."

About quilting in general, Rebekka says, "Being married

"It may take the rest of my life for me to reach perfection in my techniques, but the trip will be fun – and well worth the effort."

PRE-PUBESCENT
POOL PARTY
110" x 88"
1990
Rebekka Seigel

to a potter and therefore steeped in the lives of craftspersons in all media, I think it is safe to say that the women who make quilts are by far the most generous, supportive, and sharing group of artists I have ever experienced. (I guess I should say women and men, since men are starting to arrive on the scene.)" Rebekka explains further, "Quilters do not guard their secrets and techniques the way other craftspeople sometimes do, but are willing to help a fellow quilter whenever they can."

Doris Waddell
Bath, Ontario, Canada

Family Album

"This quilt," says Doris Waddell, "was certainly a labor of love. Never having made so complicated a piece, I began with the easiest blocks, gradually working up to the more difficult ones. The family blocks were the most fun to do and are the most appreciated by judges. I have portrayed each of us doing a favorite activity in a familiar setting. I am the 'quilter' and in a touch of humor I included my tennis racket – my other passion."

third place

1991 AQS Show & Contest
Appliqué, Pro

Doris adds, "It was challenging choosing the fabrics – tree trunks, water, birds – all of the pieces needed to be just the right material."

Doris says her album quilt was inspired by numerous quilts she had seen in museums, in quilt shows and in books. She adds, "Several of the blocks were from Elly Sienkiewicz's book *Spoken Without a Word*, five were original blocks, and seven were from other sources, often with my own adaptations. The border appliqué and quilting designs were drafted by me to fit the scale of the blocks in the top."

FAMILY ALBUM includes a great deal of detail added with reverse appliqué and embroidery touches. For example, the calico cat in the 'quilter' block contains approximately 175 French knots. Doris comments, "The quilt took 4000 hours to complete. The two-year period I worked on it was a

time of great joy and satisfaction for me."

About her background, Doris says, "I began quilting in 1976 after viewing a local quilt show at Kingston's Agnes Etherington Art Centre. Largely self taught, I eventually attended very enlightening workshops and talks by some of North America's finest quilt artists."

Doris continues, "FAMILY ALBUM has been recognized in several books, magazines, newspapers, and slide shows, and has won other awards. Naturally this has been very gratifying to me, but I know it will be a hard act to follow in future endeavors."

Asked why she feels quilting is so popular, Doris says, "Interest in quiltmaking has been piqued by the many quilt shows and competitions, the books and magazines featuring today's quilts and quiltmakers, and the willingness of quilters everywhere to show their work and share their expertise. I would guess that in no other art or craft network would you find so enthusiastic and cohesive a group."

*"While I thoroughly enjoy and admire 'art' quilts,
my particular forte seems to be the traditional quilt."*

FAMILY ALBUM
90" x 90"
1990
Doris Waddell

Deborah Hall
Cincinnati, Ohio

Peaceable Kingdom

About the development of this quilt, Deborah Hall says, "My interest in geometry came together with a need to produce Christmas decorations and a pile of red moire-taffeta scraps from a gown my daughter was making. I never want to piece with taffeta again, but the wall-hanging I made was such a success that I started teaching a class in making my Pieceful Feathered Star. I sewed parts of a red and white star as demonstration pieces in my classes, then decided to make a quilt."

first place

1991 AQS Show & Contest Other Techniques

Deborah continues, "The quilt was designed from the center out, though my goal was a double-bed sized quilt with borders of little triangles. The trapunto in the center came next and was a reaction against the traditional war-like eagle. All four Feathered Stars were joined together when I decided to trapunto animals in the white spaces. I took the stars apart into nine sections so I could quilt them on the machine." She explains, "My old sewing machine does only straight stitch and I don't use a walking foot. I quilt through front, batting, and lining and then stuff yarn in with a needle, through the lining."

Speaking of the trapunto design, Deborah says, " Some of the animals were inspired by Edward Hicks' 'Peaceable Kingdom' paintings, some came from various books, and the rest I just drew." Deborah adds, "I was designing and sewing the animals on this quilt while listening to news of the fall of the Berlin Wall and the release of Nelson Mandela. My hopes for a more peaceful world are stitched into this quilt."

Deborah talks of her background: "I made a pillow inspired by a mola in 1966 and a baby quilt in 1968. My first big quilt (a Lone Star) was 12 years in the making. I didn't meet another quilter until 1981 when the Ohio Valley Quilter's Guild was formed. I am mostly self-taught and often decide to do something just to see if it can be done." She adds, "The most consistent element in my quilts is a love of the color red and a fondness for tiny triangles."

About PEACEABLE KINGDOM, Deborah says, "The quilt inspired me to enter Expo Europa II where it took a first prize, to travel to Denmark, and also to go to our Sister City, Kharkiv, in Ukraine, to teach quiltmaking. That led to my starting The Kharkiv Project in the Ohio Valley Quilter's Guild. We are bringing two excellent Ukranian quilters (husband and wife) to Cincinnati as a direct result of my trip. I am so very interested in international exchange in the quilt world."

About quilting, Deborah comments, "Quilting offers us more opportunities to connect with each other and with our own deepest feelings than other needlearts do – partly because of the traditional use of quilts on beds and their connections with birth, marriage, and death. The materials used in quilts add layers of meaning, too – no other needlework offers the possibilities of the charm quilt, the friendship quilt, or

"I don't want to make another quilt this complicated again, but I may eat my words if I get another inspiration."

PEACEABLE
KINGDOM
72" x 88"
1990
Deborah Hall

quilts made of favorite, but now outgrown garments; no other needlework has the history of the quilting bee. Quilting truly brings us together!"

Annabel Baugher
Galt, Missouri

Arabesque

Annabel Baugher comments, "The first inspiration for ARABESQUE was an 1830 French print included in the book *Baltimore Album Quilts* published by the Baltimore Museum. When I saw it, the first thing that entered my mind was 'I could quilt that.' "

Annabel continues, "Since I do not draw freehand I am very happy new technology

second place

*1991 AQS Show & Contest
Other Techniques*

provides me with photocopy machines and opaque projectors. Once the picture was drawn to size, I began manipulating it, taking a bit off here – adding a leaf or flower there – setting a scroll at a new angle. Finally I had converted the overall shape to a diamond. I placed it in an oval and added beading to form the oval."

Continuing, Annabel says, "To make the beading design I drew around a dime. The border around the central design is the embossing on a Mother's Day card given to

me many years ago. This center section was on paper quite some time before I came up with an appropriate border design. Then, in a magazine I spied just the border I was looking for."

Annabel reveals that ARABESQUE was almost half quilted before it had a name. "I was looking up a word in the dictionary when I saw a picture resembling the border of my quilt. Beneath it was the word 'arabesque.' The definition simply said 'Arabic art.' My quilt at last had a name."

Annabel used muslin on the back of this quilt, to

make the trapunto easier. The quilt required 3,000 yards of quilting thread because of the amount of stipple quilting. Acrylic yarn and small strips of batting were inserted into the trapunto with a tapestry needle.

Describing her background, Annabel says, "I do not remember when the first needle was placed in my hand and thimble put on my finger. My mother saw to it that I learned good hand sewing skills." Annabel continues, "I've really enjoyed making quilts for my family. I have never made a quilt for myself – that just doesn't have the same appeal." She adds, "I live on the farm where I've lived for 50 years and enjoy gardening, reading and teaching others this wonderful art of quiltmaking."

Annabel says she would most like people to know that "ARABESQUE was exciting from the first inspiration to the last stitch, though many months passed between." She adds, "As each segment fell into place the design appealed to me more. The techniques of stippling and trapunto are time-consuming,

"I started to quilt quite by accident. My daughter-in-law wanted a quilted bedspread, and I consented to make one."

ARABESQUE
96" x 99"
1990
Annabel
Baugher

but also very rewarding – they bring designs out into a much bolder relief." She adds, "This quilt was made for my only Grandson."

Asked why she thinks quilting is so popular today, Annabel replies, "Because quilts have been lifted from the realm of utilitarian to the realm of art. This came about as we began to really see the beauty our ancestors craved and achieved in even the most utilitarian of household objects. There is a yearning – a need for beauty in every person."

Carol Goddu
Mississauga, Ontario, Canada

Schools Of Modern Art

Carol Goddu's design for SCHOOLS OF MODERN ART is an original redrafting of the traditional schoolhouse block. She describes the significance of the design, "Each block is done in the style of a different nineteenth or twentieth century painter. From left to right, beginning at the top left are represented: Henri Rousseau, Piet Mondrian, Georges Seurat, Henri Matisse, René Magritte, Andy Warhol, Georgia O'Keeffe, Henri de Toulouse-Lautrec, Vincent Van Gogh, Claude Monet, Jackson Pollock, and Pablo Picasso (during his blue period)."

third place

1991 AQS Show & Contest
Other Techniques

The quilt is machine pieced, machine quilted, hand and machine appliquéd in cottons, synthetics and Ultra-Suede®. The quilt also includes hand-painted, hand-dyed, xeroxed and marbleized cottons. Carol adds, "The borders provided an opportunity for me to also include an assortment of wild painterly prints."

Carol has been quilting since 1972, when she began working with traditional patchwork patterns. In 1981 she started working in pictorial appliqué, and began exhibiting her work in 1983. Her quilts have appeared in many juried shows and exhibits, and also in a number of publications.

Asked if she would do anything differently if beginning the quilt today, Carol says she would not. She then adds, "I might, though, come back to this subject and try making blocks in earlier artists' styles. I haven't done any blocks with artists working before the impressionists, so there must be at least one more art school quilt waiting to be made."

About her award, Carol says, "This quilt was rejected by the first juried show to which it was submitted, but at its next show, the annual AQS show, it was not only accepted for display but was also selected as a prizewinner. This certainly suggests that no single jury should have the final word on a quilter's work; it really does pay to get a second opinion."

About the current popularity of quilting, Carol says, "I certainly find more satis-

"Having tried weaving, knitting, needlepoint, cross-stitch, and other needlearts, I have discovered I find more enjoyment in working with pieces of fabric than I do in manipulating lengths of thread."

SCHOOLS OF
MODERN ART
78" x 81"
1990
Carol Goddu

faction in any one of my needlearts than I ever found in baking or cooking. Turn out a masterpiece in the kitchen and the highest compliment people can pay is to eat it all up. At least when you slave over a quilt it has some permanence and brings pleasure to the viewer and satisfaction to the maker for many years to come."

Faye Anderson
Boulder, Colorado

R.E.M. (Rapid Eye Movement)

"I could be accused of being lazy," comments Faye Anderson, "but I try to think of my penchant for catnaps and daydreaming as my creative time. Whenever I am stumped on a design problem, the solution comes to me as I am falling asleep or just as I wake up. As a result, I wanted to do a quilt about sleep, specifically R.E.M (rapid eye movement) sleep, the time when the mind goes through the day's information and sorts and stores it for future use."

first place

1991 AQS Show & Contest Theme: Stars

Faye explains that the quilt is mainly appliquéd: "Most quilters would piece stars and zigzags, but I find them easier to appliqué. I use direct, no-baste, needle-turn appliqué, done flat on a board, which helps the final work lie flat and not pucker." Faye adds. "Debra Lunn's hand-dyed fabrics were used in the color wheel zigzag border."

Speaking of her background, Faye says, "I began quilting in 1980. Involved in a small way in the buying and selling of investment real estate, I bought a commercial building next to a quilt shop. I wandered into the quilt shop, signed up for a sampler class, and was hooked. I gave up real estate and haven't been far from a needle and thread ever since."

Asked what she would like people to know about this quilt, Faye says, "This is a complicated looking design and its development was difficult, but it was not painful! The quilt was finished for the

star theme category, but it was not started with that in mind." Faye explains, "The center star section was made as a beginning for a quilt based on Don McLean's song about Vincent Van Gogh, 'Starry Starry Night.' I was making the quilt for the music quilt competition at Quilting-by-the-Lake. Elaborate appliqué borders were added and the results were gloomy and morbid."

Faye continues, "I had other things to work on, so I put the pieces away in a dark closet. About 18 months later, when I had more time, I pulled them out and let the project take over my living room – it seemed to want to be a *BIG* quilt, so I needed a bigger room than my studio to study the design. I used stacks of fabric and drawing paper as I worked out the borders. Each problem was solved by living with the quilt's presence in my living room. The solutions came to me in daydreams and sleep. It was an interesting creative experience for me."

Asked if she would do anything differently if beginning the quilt now, Faye says,

"This quilt was used on a New Year's card. It hadn't occurred to me that it had a mood of celebration and fireworks – I am happy a design that started out 'gloomy and morbid' was able to become festive!"

R.E.M.
(RAPID EYE
MOVEMENT)
98" x 102"
©1991
Faye Anderson

"Hopefully I would do everything differently! The design process was disjointed and difficult. I learned a lot, but I wouldn't look forward to doing things the 'hard way' in the future!"

About today's interest in quiltmaking, Faye says, "I think the potential for networking is important. What started as the quilting bee, getting together with neighbors and church friends, has become a common thread for women and men around the world. The sewing is only one part of the picture. Getting involved in the quilt community enriches one's life enormously."

Kathleen H. McCrady
Austin, Texas

Six x Six Comes Up Roses

Speaking of the development of this quilt, Kathleen McCrady says, "In books I had seen many 1850-1885 quilts that had medallion centers and lots of pieced borders. I had always wanted to someday create that kind of quilt. An acquaintance returned from conserving a quilt that belonged to the Long Island Historical Society. She shared a black and white photo of the quilt with me, and the center fascinated me. One day I took the photo to a copy machine, enlarged it, and colored in areas for background piecing."

second place

1991 AQS Show & Contest Theme: Stars

The design was underway. She explains, "Drafting a six-pointed star in the round is not difficult, but piecing adjoining stars accurately requires skilled hands. I know now why there are not many quilts with this type of piecing." Kathleen continues, "After piecing the center, I labored over what to do next. I settled on a setting with *broderie perse* roses appliquéd around the center. A Sawtooth border seemed appropriate to frame it. I pieced several examples of borders with lots of little pieces. Most did not work! Finally I decided that the little six-pointed stars would look nice with the other pieced border. Adding a larger star to the corners helped me turn the corners, and repeating the appliqué in the final pieced border added interest."

Making this quilt involved drafting, hand piecing, *broderie perse*, appliqué, and hand quilting. Kathleen adds that the only portion of this quilt based on another quilt is the center portion.

Kathleen is a third generation Texas quiltmaker. She comments, "I grew up in a home where quilts were made for cover, quilted on a frame suspended from the ceiling. I learned to quilt as a teenager on quilts my mother made. When I married, I acquired another quiltmaking connection: my mother-in-law and I shared quilting for more than 40 years. It was she and her mother who gave me the quilt tops I quilted soon after I was married. I loved the quilting process, but at first I did not want to piece quilts. All I knew were scrap quilts, utility quilts made for cover. One of my first piecing experiences was a Lone Star quilt made from fabrics I purchased."

Continuing to talk about her background, Kathleen says, "I quilted during the dry years – 1950-1970. Having moved from a rural farm community to an urban area, I did not have contact with other quiltmakers. Women my age who had young families did not quilt – they bought blankets! With a busy family, quilts I created during that time were traditional quilts. It was not until I became associated with organized quiltmaking in the late 1970's that I learned new techniques, how to draft patterns, and how to use fabric and colors in creative ways."

Kathleen has been teaching quiltmaking for almost 12 years, and her quilts have won many honors.

"This quilt," Kathleen explains, "was not planned

"Our appetites are whetted by the wonderful array of fabrics available to the quiltmaker today. I remember in 1973 trying to find 100% cotton to finish a quilt. It was like looking for a needle in a haystack."

SIX X SIX
COMES UP
ROSES
107" x 87"
1990
Kathleen H.
McCrady

out. It was planned as it went along." Asked if she would do anything differently if beginning her quilt today, Kathleen says, "I would probably draw it out, at least partially."

Commenting on her AQS award, Kathleen says, "Sometimes when I look at this quilt, I wonder how I did it! It has given me a great deal of satisfaction knowing I could produce a quilt that has received the award from AQS as well as awards in a number of other shows."

About current interest in quilting, Kathleen says, "My own interest in quiltmaking is great because it fulfills a creative need. There is also something very therapeutic about the sewing and quilting process. No other media can give the same feeling of creative satisfaction that comes from making a quilt."

143

Isolde Sarnecki de Vries
Ann Arbor, Michigan

Cosmos (In Honor Of Hercules Who Still Looks Spiffy After All These Years)

Isolde Sarnecki de Vries says of the inspiration for this quilt, "I made the quilt after I saw a postcard with a starry design. I modified the stars and airbrushed the constellations behind them. Then I added the earth, the wind, and the sunburst."

third place

1991 AQS Show & Contest Theme: Stars

The quilt involves a number of different techniques – appliqué, piecing, painting, and embroidery – and a range of materials – cottons, lamés, textile paints, paint canvas, and various embroidery threads.

Speaking about the meaning of the elements of the design, Isolde comments, "The quilt depicts the four seasons, and the wind, the sun, and the moon. It also depicts eagles and buffaloes, which stand as symbols of man's contempt for nature." She continues, "The earth is surrounded by dying trees, to remind us of the fragility of our planet." Asked if she would do anything differently if beginning the quilt today, Isolde replies that she does not think she would.

Commenting on her background and her interest in quilting, Isolde says, "Since I saw my first quilts 15 years ago I have been attracted to their powerful graphic design qualities, but I did not start making quilts myself until I saw the first television series on quilting, which was hosted by Penny McMorris.

That was in 1985. On one of the programs in that series I saw contemporary quilts by Jan Meyers-Newbury, Terrie Mangat, and Michael James, and I was just flabbergasted."

Asked why she feels quilting is enjoying such great popularity today, Isolde replies, "Quilts are perceived to be a non-threatening tactile medium, which makes them very appealing. People who would never be caught in an art museum will go to a quilt exhibit in that very same museum." Isolde says she finds the "bickering among the 'traditionalists' and the 'non-traditionalists' sometimes disheartening." Though an avid quiltmaker, Isolde also continues to work in other media: "I enjoy working with watercolor and collage as well."

"COSMOS is a 'green' quilt. It was made to celebrate the work of human and divine hands."

COSMOS
72" x 95"
1991
Isolde Sarnecki
de Vries

Patricia B. Campbell
Dallas, Texas

Elizabethan Woods

Speaking about the development of this quilt, Patricia B. Campbell says, "This quilt was inspired by a seventeenth century bed hanging with Elizabethan swirls, which were done in crewel embroidery using wools on linen." Patricia adds, "The idea to leave the center oval open for quilting came from a table cover."

first place

*1991 AQS Show & Contest
Group/Team*

The top of this quilt was hand appliquéd using a wide variety of commercial prints and purchased hand-dyed fabrics, and joined to the back with a low loft batt.

Commenting on her own background, Patricia says, "I did not learn quiltmaking from my mother or grandmother. Neither was a needlewoman, but my mother did give me her thimble when I was 15. I think she knew that someday I'd put it to good use." Patricia adds, "I don't have formal training in art and I've never taken color

or design classes. I don't even quilt very well. I appliqué. I tell my students that if I can stitch exciting quilts without years of study, so can they."

Patricia explains, "ELIZABETHAN WOODS combines a series of design and needlework challenges in executing an oval of curves, the same type of challenges that quiltmakers through the ages have thrived on. The oval of Elizabethan circular vines holds the fantasy flowers and leaves of another century's needlework, carefully colored

to resemble the soft tones of hand-dyed wools. This piece borrows its motifs from the strong crewel embroidery elements of the wonderful bed hangings of two and three centuries ago, carrying on the strong quiltmaking/artist tradition of 'borrowing' from other media and then presenting this beauty in a new way."

Asked if she might do anything differently if beginning this quilt today, Patricia replies, "I might try to create this quilt on one cloth piece. It was technically difficult working with four quadrants, and piecing them together required total concentration. However, I would not change the design elements." Patricia feels this quilt "added interest to the botanical fantasies of the Jacobean era."

Asked to comment on quilting in general, Patricia says, "Occasionally, during a workshop, a quiltmaker will express a bit of guilt with regard to her fabric and notions purchases. I tell her to see me at lunch break so we can discuss her husband's hobbies. This always brings a smile to her face!"

Patricia B. Campbell: "Quilts and quiltmaking inspire creativity, and guilds and shows stimulate our minds and our hearts."

ELIZABETHAN
WOODS
68" x 84"
©1991
Patricia B.
Campbell

Quilted by
Thekla
Schnitker

Sandra Heyman, Burns, Kansas
Linda Nonken, El Dorado, Kansas

Sticks And Twigs

Speaking of the development of this quilt, Linda Nonken comments, "With STICKS AND TWIGS we were interested in creating a contemporary version of a Baltimore Album style quilt. One of our major concerns in doing so was that we keep the layering of fabric to a minimum, to facilitate quilting. Clear colors were added to the traditional red and green to add intensity."

second place

1991 AQS Show & Contest Group/Team

Describing the construction, Linda says, "Cutout blocks were designed by the paper cut technique. Grapes and cherries were appliquéd with the freezer paper method, and the trailing stems were created with bias strips. The heart stems are cut-work appliqué." The hand quilting design involved different patterns: the background is cross-hatched; the sashing is cable quilted; and the shapes are outline quilted.

Linda says she and Sandy very much enjoy working together. She elaborates: "This is our eighth competition quilt together, and as with all the others, we shared the work equally – and each grew with the experience. Our research into album style quilts was rewarding."

Sandy's and Linda's families have been friends for years – Sandy grew up in the same small community as Linda's husband. Sandy's first contact with quilting was through her grandmother, who quilted for a living. Linda, on the other hand, was first introduced to quilting through an article on English paper piecing in an issue of *Golden Hands* magazine that she picked up at the grocery store. Linda was intrigued and began playing around with quilting.

Sandy and Linda were out shopping one day when Sandy mentioned that she would like to have a quilt for an antique bed she was inheriting. Linda offered to help Sandy make the quilt, limited as her experience was. Linda comments, "We had no idea what we were getting into. That first quilt

Left: Sandra Heyman, right: Linda Nonken

148

Linda Nonken: "I think we work together so well because we trust each other. We know we can depend on quality work, no matter for whom the quilt is intended."

STICKS AND
TWIGS
87" x 87"
1991
Sandra Heyman
& Linda Nonken

was a white-work quilt, with lace trim. We even tatted the 17 yards of lace needed." But, these two women have continued to quilt together: "We have made a quilt each year since then, each of us receiving the quilt alternate years."

In a spirit of true collaboration, Sandy and Linda are usually discussing the design of the next quilt as they are quilting the one now underway. They each participate in all aspects. When they began their first project they determined the number of stitches per inch they would do and measured often. The method succeeded. Linda comments, "We work so closely together that it is often difficult for even the two of us to tell where one person left off and

Chime Saltz, Pulaski, Virginia
& Wendy Crigger, Wytheville, Virginia

In The Bleak Midwinter

Chime Saltz says, "I designed the block in a Quilts in a Series session with Nancy Crow at Arrowmont School of Arts and Crafts in Gatlinburg, Tennessee. Later, I redrew the entire setting and selected the fabrics." She adds, "I deliberately chose black, white, and gray because of their strong value contrast."

third place

1991 AQS Show & Contest Group/Team

The top is machine pieced, and the piping has a strand of acrylic yarn pulled through it. Wendy Crigger, who quilted the top adds, "In most cases the quilting lines mimic the print of the fabrics. It was a challenge to keep coming up with differnt patterns for the pin-dot and solid areas."

Chime says she "was introduced to quilting by the ladies of the Blue Ridge Institute at Ferrum College in Ferrum, Virginia." Wendy began quilting in 1986 after having taken a class at the local fabric store. She comments, "I felt it was a good way to leave a legacy that would be different from that of others my age."

Asked what she would like people to know about this quilt, Chime says, "I feel use of value is one of the most important aspects of design, so I have spent the past three years working in black and white. I feel very pleased with my growth." Wendy says, "None of the quilting lines were marked. Everything was done freehand. Quilters shouldn't be afraid to just start and see where they finish." She adds, "I will always be grateful to Chime for giving me the opportunity to contribute to this beautiful quilt."

Speaking on the popularity of quilting, Chime says, "I think almost everybody identifies with quilts. I always carry something to work on during times I may have to wait. When people see me working they always want to share some aspect of quilting with me. On the whole, quilters are a sharing and generous community."

Wendy adds, "I think people are trying to get back to basics, and this is one area where that is possible. There is a new appreciation of handwork and the great amount of time it involves, and people are seeing quilts as the works of art they have been for generations. For me, quilting is a common bond with those who came before me and with those who will come after me."

Chime Saltz

Wendy Crigger

Chime Saltz: "I never cease to be amazed by the innovations and contributions made by quilters."
Wendy Crigger: "I'm proud to be doing my part to see that the tradition of quilts continues."

IN THE BLEAK
MIDWINTER
71" x 86"
1990
Chime Saltz

Quilted by
Wendy Crigger

Alison Goss
Hockessin, Delaware

Ancient Directions

In discussing the development of ANCIENT DIRECTIONS, Alison Goss says, "This quilt was inspired by the black and white fine-line designs of Pueblo Indian pottery, and an appreciation for the indigenous cultures of the American Southwest, whose people have lived for centuries in harmony and in balance with the land."

best wall quilt

1991 AQS Show & Contest

This quilt is made of all-cotton fabrics, including plaids, ikats, hand-painted fabrics– some painted by Alison and some purchased – and marbled fabrics. Speaking of the construction Alison explains, "I used the sewing-to-paper method I have developed to make all of the pieces fit together accurately. The quilt was then free-hand machine quilted."

About her sewing and quiltmaking background, Alison says, "I made some patchwork curtains, placemats, and other things in the mid-seventies, but didn't start making quilts seriously until 1980." She adds, "I carefully avoided all art classes through high school and college because a fifth grade teacher had convinced me that I wasn't 'good at art.' "

Alison continues, "After working for ten years to develop my ability to use color and design to convey ideas and emotions, I felt that I had finally made a breakthrough with this quilt." She adds, "Creative inspiration doesn't come to me like a 'bolt out of the blue.' Rather, it comes as a result of a very gradual process of learning from and building upon previous work."

Asked if she would do anything differently if beginning this quilt today, Alison replies, "I am currently working on a series exploring variations in the use of the central image and the space surrounding it, so rather than thinking in terms of changing ANCIENT DIRECTIONS, I think of continuing to try different design ideas in new quilts."

"I felt that this quilt was a breakthrough for me, so completing it was an affirmation that I was headed in the right direction with my work."

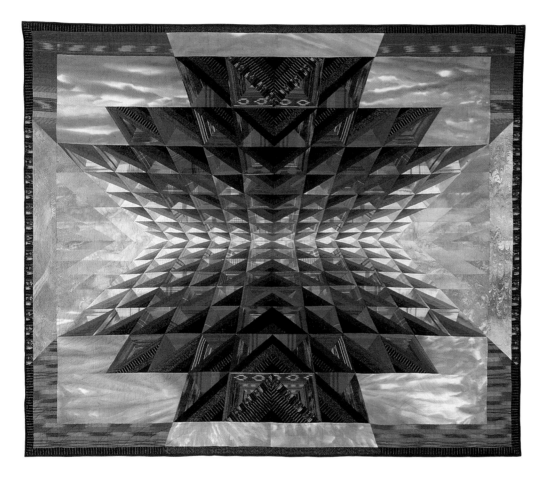

ANCIENT
DIRECTIONS
80" x 67"
©1990
Alison Goss

Museum of AQS Collection

Of her AQS Show award, Alison says, "The award was totally unexpected, and a very exciting and gratifying form of recognition, one which has given me the opportunity to share my work with many more quilters."

About quilting Alison comments, "Quiltmaking is a very accessible medium for creative expression. Quilt-makers at every level of experience get excited about creating something new and different, whether they're making bed quilts as gifts for family and friends, or 'studio quilts' as art for the wall. I may be biased, but I have found that the people who choose to make quilts share a lot of wonderful qualities – they are warm, friendly people who are always willing to share and interested in exploring new ideas."

Lynn J. Crook
Berkeley, California

The Red Window

THE RED WINDOW is part of a series of quilts Lynn J. Crook has been making. She explains, "Since I first began to create my own quilt designs in 1987, I have been using a nine-block grid based on the traditional Sawtooth block as a beginning point. Using the same Sawtooth grid as a beginning for each quilt allows me to explore new ideas in the next by using different colors, themes, quilt lines, and fabrics."

first place

1991 AQS Show & Contest Wall Quilt, Amateur

Lynn continues, "I like the dynamics of the triangle counterpointed by the symmetry of the large squares. As I design, I turn the large square into different patterns. THE RED WINDOW was the fifth quilt in the series, and in it I wanted to return to the exclusive use of solid-colored cottons. The result is a stronger graphic design.

"In THE RED WINDOW," explains Lynn, "the large squares of the traditional Sawtooth become a window with the sashing in red, an outer frame of violet, and small navy blue corners – the glass through which one views deep space or night. The Sawtooth triangles merged with one another to become four large bands crisscrossing the window. Strip piecing further emphasized the diagonal of the triangles and played up the color interaction."

Speaking of her inspiration, Lynn says, "I have had the opportunity through East Bay Heritage Quilters to learn from numerous quilters, all of whom have added to my knowledge of the endless possibilities in the quilting medium. I feel this quilt especially reflects the inspiration I received from the quilts of Michael James and the Amish."

About her background, Lynn says, "I had worked with many art materials, particularly oils and acrylic paints, since my childhood. During that time I had also done many needlework projects, from cross-stitch to macramé, to clothing. Quilting is a wonderful marriage of all these pursuits. I began quilting while working on a school raffle quilt project for my children's elementary school. The women involved were a wonderfully creative, talented, and welcoming group, and they introduced me to the large and vibrant organization, East Bay Heritage Quilters. Then, while taking an art class at a junior college, the instructor shared an article on art quilts. Seeing this, I felt comfortable creating my class project in quilt form – I was hooked."

Asked why there is such

"I like the quilting to be an active part of the quilt design, adding texture and another dimension."

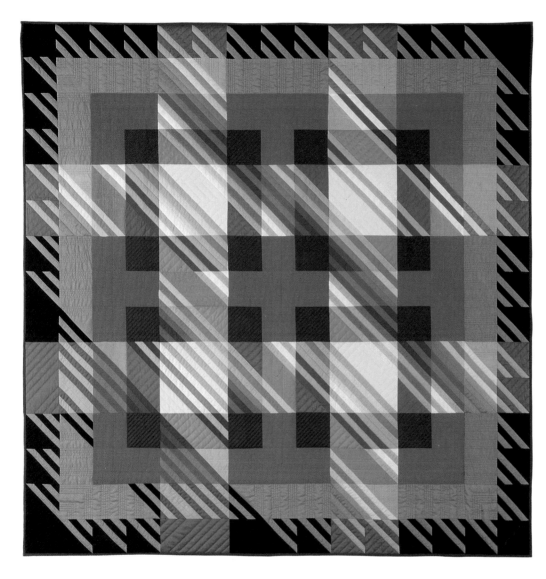

THE RED
WINDOW
62" x 62"
1990
Lynn J. Crook

interest in quilting, Lynn says, "I think there are many reasons for the quilt revival. People feel comfortable around quilts; they are familiar and approachable. The range of styles – traditional through contemporary – and the broad usage – bed covers through wallhangings – makes quilting appealing to a broad audience and to a large group of creators. Quilting is house friendly, meaning that one can do the work in the home under many different circumstances. It doesn't require a lot of expensive equipment or a large space the way that many other art activities do."

Adrien Rothschild
Baltimore, Maryland

Genetic Engineering Brings You Designer Christmas Trees

"The block design used in this quilt," explains Adrien Rothschild, "was inspired by an experience when I was bicycling in New Zealand. It is the same block I used in my quilt IT SNOWED ON THE MOUNTAIN LAST NIGHT – but used with different colors. I liked the design and wanted to use it again to see what other effects I could achieve using different colors. Most of my quilts are created because I want to see what happens when colors are used in other ways."

second place

1991 AQS Show & Contest Wall Quilt, Amateur

Adrien adds, "I was very pleased with the results. In the original quilt using the design the colors were simpler; each tree was one solid color. In this quilt each of the branches or logs grade, so there are five gradations of hand-dyed cottons used in each tree. This gradation of color creates a shimmering effect I really like. This quilt has been very popular, and I must admit that it's as pleasing to me as it apparently is to others."

Asked about the title, Adrien explains, "The name came in response to what I saw. Rarely do I name my quilts in advance. The names come after seeing what I have done. In this case, I thought – these days it's designer jeans, designer this, designer that. Why not Christmas trees, color-coordinated with livingroom decor?"

Adrien began quilting in 1978: "I intended to make just one quilt for my bed. I was inspired by awareness of a renewed interest in quilts." Adrien has since made over forty quilts, but she adds, "Bicycling is my foremost passion. Quiltmaking is number two."

Winning awards has given her much self-confidence. She comments, "It is nice to know that my work is good and that it measures up in competition. Awards also mean my phone rings more often, but they haven't really changed my work."

Adrien enjoys entering juried shows. "It would be hard to keep going without them. I particularly enjoy judged shows." Asked why, she replies, "Because like everyone else, I enjoy spending money. The money I have earned in 1992 I'm spending on a return trip to New Zealand." She adds, "While there I'm doing a lecture tour and will be meeting quilters throughout the country."

She will also be doing some teaching for the first time. "I have never wanted to teach because I have never thought it was a good idea to copy or to do someone else's idea." Adrien explains her current plans to teach: "Some of the quilters I've talked with in Tasmania, where I'm also going on my trip, asked me to bring freezer paper. They have heard of but have never used it. I taught myself how to use it when I was doing some appliqué (work which only the ladies in my quilt circle have seen), so I will be teaching these quilters how to use the paper I'm bringing."

Asked why she thinks she stopped painting and began quilting, Adrien says that she feels the answer may parallel the reason Josef Albers used

*"I like this quilt a lot – the colors are fun.
My main enjoyment in making quilts is working with color."*

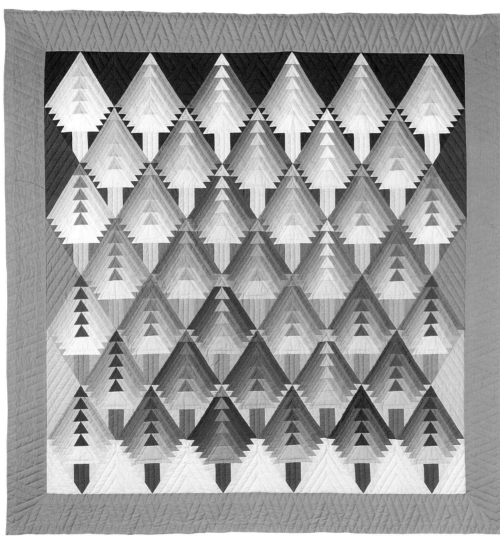

GENETIC
ENGINEERING
BRINGS YOU
DESIGNER
CHRISTMAS
TREES
62" x 62"
©1990
Adrien
Rothschild

Photo: Aaron M. Levin

pieces of paper instead of paints to teach color. "You can't ever re-create the exact same color with pigments, but pieces of a length of fabric will be the same color. I work with fabric in much the way that one can explore color using paper and Josef Albers' exercises. Color and light are very important to me. That's probably why I make quilts at all and why I make the specific kinds of quilts that I do."

Nancy S. Brown
Oakland, California

In A Galaxy Far, Far, Far, Far, Far Away

To explain the development of this award-winning quilt, Nancy S. Brown refers back to another of her quilts: "When I designed THE ANIMAL ALPHABET QUILT, the animal illustrating X was an imaginary creature. I had great fun designing that animal, and it received many comments, so I decided to make an entire quilt of imaginary animals." Nancy adds,

third place

1991 AQS Show & Contest Wall Quilt, Amateur

"Since I have always enjoyed science fiction stories about outer space, I decided these imaginary animals would be from outer space and I would use that theme in the border."

Asked what she would like people to know about this quilt, Nancy says, "When people find out that all of the quilt's outer space animals are created from parts of actual animals, they seem to enjoy guessing which animals make up the various creatures. The color and size of the part may be changed

so it isn't always easy to guess its origin."

Speaking of the quilt's construction, Nancy explains, "It was hand appliquéd and quilted – the blocks were lap quilted and then pieced together by machine. In the borders are rhinestone moons and stars and several old buttons that look like planets and meteors. There are also many different colored small beads throughout the quilt, and the borders are quilted with metallic thread." Nancy adds, "Fabric paint was used to create the shooting stars and distant galaxies

in the borders."

Of her background Nancy says, "My mother taught me to quilt after taking a class but later I discovered there were quilters on both sides of the family. My great grandmother quilted and my great uncle made quilts for a living after he was injured in a farming accident. I wish I could have met them."

Asked if she would change anything if she were beginning this quilt today, Nancy talks about the embellishments. "All of the beading, rhinestones and metallic thread were used so the quilt would sparkle like the night sky. Unfortunately, except in certain light, they don't really work. I would never take them off this quilt, but I'm not sure I would use them in another."

About the effects of winning an award, Nancy says, "It has been very encouraging to have one of my quilts recognized by such a prestigious organization. Also, by going to the show, I have discovered an absolutely wonderful city in Paducah, a city that goes all out to welcome quilters."

"Quiltmaking is like a contagious disease. Once you come into contact with enthusiastic quilters, beautiful fabric, and creative patterns, you are infected and there's no cure – but who wants one anyway?"

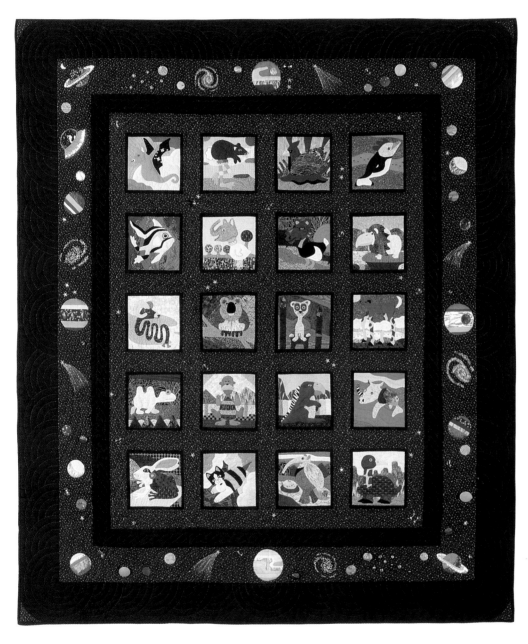

IN A GALAXY
FAR, FAR, FAR,
FAR, FAR AWAY
56" x 65"
1990
Nancy S. Brown

Jane Blair
Wyomissing, Pennsylvania

Continuum

Jane Blair explains that CONTINUUM "is an original design which was made for The Dairy Barn's Fabric Gardens show," though the contest's jurors chose another of her quilts for inclusion in that traveling exhibition. Jane comments, "Although I thought they were wrong in their choice, their decision made CONTINUUM available for three other shows."

first place

1991 AQS Show & Contest
Wall Quilt, Professional

She adds, "The quilt won first place in the Mid-Atlantic show, for Scrap Quilt; first place at the Houston AIQA show, for Interpretive Pieced; and first place at American Quilter's Society Show, for Wall Quilt. So you see, a rejection may simply mean that your quilt hasn't fit into a specific mold. Don't blame the round peg – the problem may be the square hole. Please yourself and let others find a place for you. It's important to believe in yourself and your own ideas."

Speaking of the development of the design, Jane says, "CONTINUUM is a variation of the Nine Patch, Log Cabin and Hosanna blocks, and it represents the life cycle of a garden and of man – from the stony foundation, through roots, leaves, and flowers, to seeds and sky."

Jane adds, "I try to use only prints in my work because I like the depth and interest they add. This was a very enjoyable exercise in color, pattern and fabric placement." Jane has one last comment about the quilt: "It will be difficult to top the universal appeal of this quilt!"

Asked to comment on the current popularity of quilt-making, Jane says, "Needle-point and embroidery are stitches, painting is drawing and colors, sculpture is shape and shadow, mathematics is numbers and problems, engineering is drafting and angles; but quilting has it all! If you want a challenge or just want busy work – make a quilt. Whatever you are and whatever you like can be expressed in a quilt. No other single art form can demand so much or so little for success. It is no wonder that people find it addictive."

*"Perhaps CONTINUUM is the flower of my life cycle – perhaps not.
There are still buds in my brain that may open into other flowers in time."*

CONTINUUM
60" x 72"
1990
Jane Blair

Carol H. Gersen
Boonsboro, Maryland

Squares And Bars

Carol H. Gersen says that among the inspirations for SQUARES AND BARS were "the 1988 Presidential election campaign, moving to a house with a flagpole and a state with a wonderful flag (Maryland), 4,000 tiny squares left from a past project, and the use of the U.S. flag in American folk art." Carol explains that this quilt did not originate in a class, nor was it based on a pattern; instead, it was influenced by the work of Jan Myers-Newbury.

second place

1991 AQS Show & Contest Wall Quilt, Professional

The quilt is constructed of machine-pieced cottons, some hand dyed by the artist with fiber reactive dyes, and is machine and hand quilted. Carol comments, "It was fun to make. The rectangle at the upper left of our flag is called the union. In my quilt each union is composed of 48 squares, often arranged in gradation. The stripes are alternating solid grays with pieced strips using only those colors found in each flag's union." Carol adds, "None of this quilt is strip pieced. I wanted control over the color placement for each flag. However, there *is* a lot of randomness in this piece. Rather than being made ahead of time, decisions were made as the quilt was sewn together. Sketching and value studies were not done for this quilt."

Carol explains that she began quilting in an informal class taught by a friend in Philadelphia in the mid-1970's. "I completed my first bed-size quilt in 1979. I received a B.F.A. degree from Moore College of Art in Philadelphia in 1969 and worked as a corporate interior designer in Philadelphia for eight years. I started making quilts when my husband, my daughter and I moved to rural Maine in 1977."

Carol continues, "My dedication to this art form began in earnest after I attended a three-week workshop taught by Nancy Halpern at the Haystack School in Maine. Then in 1986, I received a work/study grant at Haystack to attend a Jan Myers-Newbury workshop on fabric dyeing and quiltmaking."

Describing her work, Carol says, "My work consists of pieced art quilts, often based on traditional American patchwork patterns. Using simple shapes and designs allows color and value to dominate my work. Since 1986, I have gradually converted to using in my quilts only my own hand-dyed fabric, because of its superior lightfastness and unlimited color range."

Speaking about her award, Carol says, "To my surprise, SQUARES AND BARS has been my most successful quilt to date." The quilt has been was used as cover art for a college textbook, is featured on the cover of the Japanese catalog for Quilt National '91, and is used in the opening sequence of each episode of the TV series *The Great American Quilt.*

Asked why quilting is so popular, Carol replies, "Our modern world craves a link to the past." She adds, "Handwork by women of past centuries has a powerful pull for me. These women left something of themselves in their

"Using simple shapes and designs allows color and value to dominate my work."

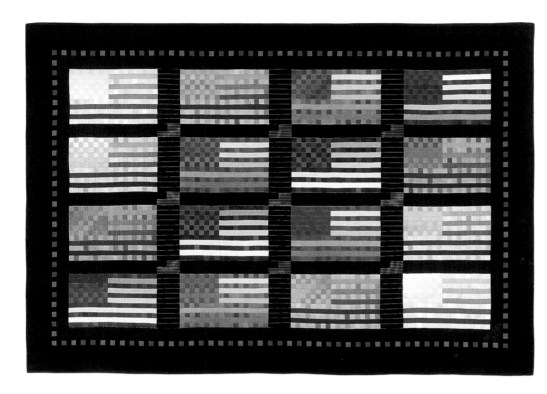

SQUARES
AND BARS
77" x 52"
©1989
Carol H.
Gersen

quilts, hooked rugs, dolls, embroidery, and clothing."

Speaking of the women in her own family, Carol says, "My grandmother tatted and embroidered. My mother made dolls, lace, embroidery and clothing. Caring for, using, and passing on these objects is important to me."

Carol doesn't believe quilting is different from other crafts: "I am not sure being involved with quilts is very different from involvement with other crafts." She explains, "Quilters are working individually, and a lot of us are interested in defining and promoting 'Studio Art Quilts.'"

Judith Reilly
Brookfield, Connecticut

Warning: Some Colors May Run

Judith Reilly explains that this quilt was the second in a series of figure quilts she made. The first she designed as a fund-raiser quilt for a community children's playground. Judith explains, "The playground quilt I made was inspired by Ruth McDowell's quilt CHERRY PEOPLE PIE (©1984). The people in Ruth's quilt were quite different from mine, but the connecting figures in her quilt are what drew me to it."

third place

1991 AQS Show & Contest Wall Quilt, Professional

About her background, Judith says, "I began quilting when I was in my teens but left it for other interests. I always had a need to be creating something and dabbled in a variety of sewing skills and crafts including tailoring, pottery, rug braiding, and basket weaving. Though I studied many art techniques in college, fabric continued to be my first love, so I returned to quilts."

Judith continues, "It is the thought process in quilt-making that fascinates me – both in designing and in determining how to technically accomplish the design." Judith adds, "It often takes me a full year to complete a quilt because the unfolding of ideas must be natural. I know that if I am patient and receptive, the right direction to take will come, and it will be better than anything I tried to force."

Speaking again about her quilt, Judith says, "This quilt was a giant stepping stone for me because it was the first quilt I designed with

every effort made to strive for a particular end result – no matter what techniques I had to use or invent to reach my goal. I really let go, and I will probably never work exclusively within the traditional framework again."

Judith does think the quilt might be different if she were beginning it today: "I have grown and learned. A quilt is never really finished in my mind. I simply have to remind myself, as I do always, that I have only one lifetime to accomplish this work. I must let go of one piece and move on to the many other ideas based on the work just completed."

Asked to comment on the current interest in quilting, Judith says, "Quiltmaking is important to me because it is a craft that is loved and appreciated by many and is acknowledged as representing home, comfort, warmth, and beauty, and it also can be a medium of infinite expression. I have explored many, many crafts and art forms through the years, and none has given me the complete satisfaction I have gained from quiltmaking."

"If you are making quilts, remember that only you really know how much progress has taken place and how much of an effect the quilt has had on your life. Every quilt that helps you grow is a winner!"

WARNING:
SOME COLORS
MAY RUN
62" x 78"
1990
Judith Reilly

Charlotte Warr Andersen
Salt Lake City, Utah

Paradise Lost

Speaking of the development of this quilt, Charlotte Warr Andersen says, "This quilt was inspired by Saltair, a resort built in 1893 on the shore of the Great Salt Lake in Utah and billed as 'The Coney Island of the West.' The Mormon Church had recently outlawed polygamy, and this was one of the ways Utahns were trying to show the rest of the country that they, too, enjoyed the American way of life. Saltair's architect was Richard Kletting, who also designed the Mormon Tabernacle. "

first place

*1991 AQS Show & Contest
Pictorial Wall Quilt*

Charlotte continues, "The resort enjoyed much success until a fire destroyed it in 1925. It was rebuilt in 1926 with a redesigned building reminiscent of the original. At one point the resort claimed to have the largest dance floor in the world, and in it's hey-day, Saltair was host to big name acts such as the Glen Miller Band and Nat

King Cole. Hard times later befell Saltair (for example, once the lake receded so that the resort was a mile from the lake's shore). The owners deeded Saltair to the State of Utah in 1959, and it sat in disrepair until it was destroyed by arson in 1970. A Saltair III was built in 1982, only to be flooded in 1984. The lake has since receded, and the current owners are trying to salvage the building."

Continuing, Charlotte adds, "I have fond memories of the second Saltair, which I visited as a small child. One of my strongest teenage fan-

tasies was to become fantastically wealthy and rebuild Saltair in all its glory. I have long since given up any hope of ever becoming wealthy enough to accomplish that feat, but making this quilt has in another way somewhat fulfilled my dream of rebuilding that PARADISE LOST."

Charlotte explains, "The pattern for the quilt was drawn using an old photograph of the building. The pattern was cut up and used for templates." The quilt was made of cottons, cotton blends, silk, acetate, rayon, nylon, lamé, and 100%

"Making one-of-a-kind pictorial quilts satisfies my need, as an artist, to create."

PARADISE LOST
80" x 66"
1989
Charlotte Warr
Andersen

polyester. It was machine pieced (except for the flags which were hand appliquéd), and then hand quilted.

Of her background, Charlotte says, "I began quilting in 1974. My first quilt was a Log Cabin done the slow way. I saw a pattern for the quilt in a magazine and set about to make one like it. It took me two years." Charlotte adds, "I haven't made a traditional quilt in a long time. I now make one-of-a-kind pictorial quilts ranging from realistic to abstract. "

Asked about the popularity of quilting, Charlotte says, "Quiltmaking has traditionally been a women's art form. I think women have a natural affinity for fabric. Personally, I have found much more satisfaction in combining fine sewing skills and design principles in my fabric pictures than I have ever derived from painting or various other forms of needlework – most of which I have taken up and put aside. Making quilts is my passion."

Barbara Lydecker Crane
Lexington, Massachusetts

Cataclysm

Barbara Lydecker Crane says that the inspiration for this original design quilt came in 1985. She elaborates, "It came from a cosmologist who issued me a lighthearted challenge to create a quilt illustrating my own view of the origin of life on earth. The idea lay at the back of my mind until I finally made CATACLYSM." Discussing the title, Barbara says, "This word can mean a 'giant upheaval,' and that is how I imagine the enormity and the mystery of life's beginnings.

second place

1991 AQS Show & Contest Pictorial Wall Quilt

The ocean and the lightning bolts denote the salt water and electricity that scientists say were likely ingredients in that 'primal soup.'"

Barbara adds, "But I hope there is also here a sense of the unknown, and perhaps of awe, to credit the hand of some larger power. Each of the six 'islands' in the quilt contain one or two fabric animals – a deer, butterflies, a

giraffe, birds, a monkey. Although my choices are hardly representative of primitive life forms, they are 100% more photogenic than amoebas or protozoans!"

This quilt is constructed of cottons, many of which are decorating fabrics. The lightning and its reflections in the water are hand-painted. In terms of techniques used, the quilt is machine-pieced, hand-appliquéd, hand-quilted and machine-quilted (with both straight and zigzag stitching used).

Barbara says, "For me, beginning a piece is the hard-

est part. I always have a definite idea or concept, but interpreting that in a visual way, translating the concept into fabric and into a quilt, is difficult." Barbara started CATACLYSM in a different style. "I was trying to make the quilt in a very abstract way, with printed fabrics intersecting, creating something new at the points where they came together. Finally I put all those scraps aside and began again, in a more literal way." Asked if she would do anything differently if starting today, Barbara replies, "If I started this

"I think there is a lot of room for quiltmakers to try to express ideas in their quilts, and not just think about nice colors and attractive designs."

CATACLYSM
77" x 41"
©1989
Barbara
Lydecker Crane

quilt all over again in a different way, I would probably just make a different mistake at first!"

About her background, Barbara says, "I have a B.S. in Fine Arts from Skidmore College. For 15 years I worked as a graphic designer, until my hobby of quiltmaking finally became my profession in 1985. In quilt art I feel I have found my voice; it is the most exciting and challenging work I have ever done. My advice to other quilt artists is, don't let anyone or anything stand in your way. Find your own voice and sing out in your quilts."

Asked about her response to winning an award, Barbara says, "It was very exciting. This was the first quilt in which I wanted to express a spiritual concept. I figured the AQS judges would either love or hate this quilt. The response to CATACLYSM made me feel that even if everyone will not agree with the idea in a quilt, it is important to present that idea. I'm pleased that my ideas can travel with my quilts."

Speaking on the popularity of quilting, Barbara says, "I always wonder if the reason working with fabrics appeals to so many people isn't that it is so neat and clean. Screen printing, for example, involves having toxic substances in the house. Oil paints smell terrible; watercolors have to be worked with quickly. And, we are less intimidated by fabrics because they're what we wrap ourselves in daily."

169

Zena Thorpe
Chatsworth, California

To England With Love

Speaking of this quilt depicting memories of her early life in England, Zena Thorpe comments, "I believe that everyone should attempt an autobiography. Sewing being my medium, this quilt is my autobiography (I was 27 when I moved to USA)."

third place

1991 AQS Show & Contest
Pictorial Wall Quilt

The pictorial quilt is hand appliquéd and hand quilted, and there is much embroidered embellishment and also crochet trim. Zena adds, "There is, though, no painting as some people think." Though the quilt is wonderfully detailed, Zena comments, "There was much more information that I wanted to get onto my quilt, but there just wasn't room. For instance, towards the end of putting it together I realized that I hadn't included any of the glorious heraldic designs that are very much a part of England's heritage. I was able to incorporate some in the quilting, but I have

decided that heraldry needs to be a whole new quilt – hence PAGEANTRY, which I suppose is a sequel to TO ENGLAND WITH LOVE.

About her background, Zena says, "I had made simple pieced quilts for the kids' beds, but did not get 'turned on' to quilting until I participated in a group commemorative quilt made to celebrate the centennial of my home town. I was asked to make a square depicting the old pioneer church. I was somewhat daunted but since the whole idea had been mine in the first place, there was no way out but to attempt to make

the block." Zena continues, "I quite surprised myself with the result – it actually looked like the pioneer church. From then on I was interested in pictorial-style quilting, and I started to see everything around me in terms of little scraps of fabric. I have often felt bewildered and even a little resentful of my obsession with tiny bits of fabric. I sometimes ask myself, 'Why am I doing this? Wouldn't it be easier and quicker to paint a picture?' But I find I want to create in the medium that has been so much a part of my development – one has to do what one has to do."

Zena has found the awards her quilt has won meaningful. She speaks of one: "TO ENGLAND WITH LOVE has had a great emotional impact on its viewers, but I was particularly gratified by the special award for workmanship that it received in England. I like the fact people enjoy it just as much up close as they do from a distance." Zena adds, "People keep telling me that I'm an artist and I keep saying, 'Oh, no. I'm a good copier and maybe an artisan, but it takes

"In this quilt I wanted to record memories of my early life in England."

TO ENGLAND
WITH LOVE
72" x 72"
1990
Zena Thorpe

someone special to be considered an artist.' However, people do seem to get pleasure from viewing my work, so I'm beginning to feel just a little bit like an artist."

Asked about quilting in general, Zena says, "I don't see quilting as being very different from other forms of artwork. If artwork is something that gives the viewer pleasure or moves his emotions in some way, then whatever accomplishes that is a valid form of art." Zena adds, "Quilt art usually also carries with it a very comfy, cozy, secure message that has great appeal in these rather unstable times."

Kathleen Etherington-Schiano
Nanuet, New York

Generations

Asked how she began the quilt, Kathleen Etherington-Schiano explains, "I started this quilt in an Amish quilt class given by Jeffery Gutcheon in 1984. I was attending with my mother. We missed the first class, but she got and gave to me the instructions – to set my design in a diamond. Thinking the instructions were for the development of a single block rather than the entire quilt, I developed the blocks in this quilt, and set them on-point. I would have made a totally different quilt had I attended that first class!"

first quilt award

1991 AQS Show & Contest

Kathleen says she has "always appreciated quilts." She explains, "As a small child I had a quilt my grandmother had made me. I guess that is what started my love for quilts. This same grandmother had taught me to sew, but I really came to quilting from more of an art background. I attended a high school for the arts in New York City, and always intended to become involved in fashion design."

This background was of assistance as Kathleen developed GENERATIONS. She explains, "At the time I was sure I was only going to ever make one quilt. I liked the Roman Stripes pattern, but I also wanted to use a Flower Basket design. My grandmother had learned to sew by making Flower Basket blocks. Thinking I would have no other opportunity to use either block, I included both of them, using my graphic design training to

combine the two."

Considering the development of the actual quilt, Kathleen explains, "This quilt took me five years to complete, and during that time many things occurred in my life: I had two wonderful children and a miscarriage, and my then 15-month-old son John required open heart surgery. (He's fine now.) This quilt was very therapeutic for me. It gave me something positive that I had control over when there was nothing I could do about other circumstances. This quilt's completion became an end or closure to the incidents I just mentioned."

Kathleen has continued to make quilts and had others in AQS shows. She comments, "I won an Honorable Mention award in 1992 – that quilt took me only one-and-a-half years to make!"

Asked why she feels quilting has become so popular, Kathleen says, "Being involved in quilting is quite different from being involved in other crafts. Most of the arts and crafts are totally individual. Quilting is not solitary. I may work as an

"I made this quilt thinking it would be the only quilt I ever made."

GENERATIONS
78" x 90"
1989
Kathleen
Etherington-
Schiano

individual, but the ladies I
quilt with are supportive and
encouraging to everyone."

Dawn E. Amos
Rapid City, South Dakota

The Garden

Speaking of the inspiration for this quilt, Dawn E. Amos says, "When my grandpa died, I received two items from his estate: the Depression-ware cookie jar we had raided as kids, and a picture of Jesus in Gethsemane. I planned to someday use the picture as the starting point for a quilt, and then the war started with Iraq. Having a brother on the ship Saratoga, I found myself glued to the television set and CNN News. As a result, this is the quilt I chose to do that year. I think we all prayed a lot during that time."

Viewer's Choice

1991 AQS Show & Contest

The quilt is made of appliquéd hand-dyed fabrics. Dawn had begun dyeing her own fabrics a few years before, to achieve the subtle solid colors she wanted in her designs.

Talking about the development of the quilt, Dawn says, "When I first started the quilt I felt the most challeng-ing part was going to be creating the face. We all have our own ideas of what Jesus looked like. It took me 10 days to draw the top half of the figure. Once I had that pattern drawn, I started to draw the face." Dawn explains, "I kept in the back of my mind the decision I had made: if I could not achieve the exact face and facial expression I wanted to portray, I would go no further with the quilt." Dawn adds, "It took me over four months to complete the quilt."

Asked if there is anything Dawn would have done differently were she beginning the quilt today, she says, "I would have had a lot more of the olive branch represented in the top corner." She explains why there is so little in the quilt now: "I could not find a clear enough picture of an olive tree to be able to draw a large one, so I had to fake it." She adds that many people who don't know about her experience do not realize that the design is supposed to be an olive branch.

A drawing class was very

Dawn E. Amos and family

"I am hesitant to explain my quilts.
I don't want to limit the viewer to my own vision."

THE GARDEN
71" x 85"
1991
Dawn E. Amos

influential in Dawn's life and quilting career. Already a painter, she had thought that she was beyond Drawing I, but now acknowledges that the class proved to be very helpful. Dawn says she has not painted since she began quilting, 12 years ago, but she does still sketch. She sometimes wishes she had more formal training in color, but feels it is probably better to just follow her own instincts as a quiltmaker.

Zena Thorpe
Chatsworth, California

To England With Love

Speaking about the inspiration for this quilt, Zena says, "I wanted to make a record of my memories of my early life in England." She explains that it wasn't until she was 27 that she moved to the United States. She says, "I believe that everyone should attempt an autobiography and, sewing being my medium, this quilt is my autobiography."

Viewer's Choice

1991 AQS Show & Contest Wall Quilt

Zena's autobiography contains much information about the country of her birth. The scenes recording memories of her early life are placed on a representation of the British flag. Each corner signifies a season, starting with spring in the upper left hand corner. Some of the English cities and countryside can be seen: the London skyline, Robin Hood, and a stately home in Derbyshire. The border around the center is filet crochet with the message, "There will always be an England."

This memory quilt was made using a number of techniques: hand appliqué, hand quilting, embroidery for embellishment, and crochet trim. Zena adds that there was no painting done, though people often think that there was.

The back of the quilt, like the front, "shouts out England." In the center is a large bulldog, which Zena explains is to England what the eagle is to America. This national symbol appears against the Union Jack, the flag of England. It is obvious that much emotion went into the development of this quilt, and it has great emotional impact on viewers. Zena comments, "I am aware that TO ENGLAND WITH LOVE has a great emotional impact on its viewers, so I was particularly gratified by a special award for workmanship that it received in England. People enjoy it just as much up close as from a distance."

Zena had made "simple pieced quilts for the kids' beds," but she really didn't become fully involved in quiltmaking until she was part of a group making a commemorative quilt to celebrate her home town's centennial. When her appliquéd pioneer church turned out well, she realized she thoroughly enjoyed pictorial appliqué, and has been working in that style ever since. She sometimes questions her "obsession with nit-picking bits of fabric," but realizes that she prefers continuing to work with textiles: "I have a desire to create in the medium which has become so much a part of my development."

Asked if she would do anything differently if beginning this quilt today, Zena says, "There was much more information that I wanted to get onto my quilt, but there just wasn't room." A sequel entitled PAGEANTRY has developed since the time she completed this quilt.

About quiltmaking, she says, "I don't see quilting as being very much different from other forms of artwork." She goes on to suggest that if you think of art as being "something that gives the viewer pleasure or moves his or her emotions in some way, then whatever way that is

"Quilt art usually carries with it a very comfy, cozy, secure message that has a great appeal in these rather unstable times."

TO ENGLAND
WITH LOVE
72" x 72"
1990
Zena Thorpe

accomplished is a valid form of art." She says that she finds "people do seem to get pleasure from viewing [her] work," and she adds that she is "beginning to feel just a little bit like an artist."

INDEX/QUILTMAKERS

Amos, Dawn E. 8, 90, 174

Andersen, Charlotte Warr 166

Anderson, Faye 140

Baaklini, Joy 28

Baugher, Annabel 136

Blair, Jane 160

Brown, Becky 24

Brown, Nancy S. 70, 158

Calvert, Moneca 118

Campbell, Patricia B. 60, 146

Collins, Donna French.............68

Cosby, Beverley 16

Crane, Barbara Lydecker 168

Crew, Mary 50

Crigger, Wendy......................150

Crook, Lynn J. 154

Denenberg, Rita......................44

Dremann, Adabelle..................80

Emery, Linda Goodmon...........42

Etherington-Schiano,
      Kathleen..........................172

Fallert, Caryl Bryer 76

Gates, Cyndy 62

Gersen, Carol H. 162

Goddu, Carol 138

Goss, Alison 152

Grady, Lucy Burtschi..............12

Grow, Debbie..........................64

Hall, Deborah 134

Hartman, Barbara Oliver 32

Hatcher, Irma Gail 98

Heyman, Sandra 148

Hill, Chizuko (Hana).............110

Hitchner, Mary Kay 66

Holihan, Jane..........................54

Jevne, Agnes Holbrook............74

Johnson, Mary 124

Johnson-Srebro, Nancy 64

Karavitis, Margie T. 18

Kratz-Miller, Karen 14

Kuebler, Mary E. 52

Lalk, Sheri Wilkinson..............58

Lenz, Betty A. 26

Magaret, Pat...........................72

Mahoney, Patricia..................102

Malwitz, Marguerite Ann 82

Marshall, Suzanne 84

Mashuta, Mary 46

McBride, Dixie 128

McCrady, Kathleen H.............142

Morgan, Mary 78, 120

Muehlstein, Jackie 60

Needham, Julia Overton.....20, 96

Nonken, Linda 148

Pasquini-Masopust, Katie 34

Patriarche, Jennifer 36

Reilly, Judith 164

Robinson, Janet.....................114

Rollins, Joan 40, 86

Rothschild, Adrien 112, 156

Ryan, Mary Klett.....................62

Saltz, Chime 150

Sarnecki de Vries, Isolde........144

Schnitker, Thekla 146

Seigel, Rebekka 130

Shannon, Jonathan................122

Simmons, Lorraine E. 38

Snelling, Jan 62

Sobel, Nancy Ann 10, 94

Sogn, Judy 106

Spahn, Judy 22

Stewart, Joyce 100

Styring, Patricia L. 126

Suiter, Betty Ekern 108

Sullivan,
      Eileen Bahring............30, 116

Thorpe, Zena.................170, 176

Vredenburg, Elsie 56

Waddell, Doris.......................132

Wagner, Debra...........48, 88, 104

INDEX/QUILTS

Ancient Directions 152
Anemones 20
Animal Alphabet Soup, The 70
Arabesque 136
Autumn Nostalgia 110
Baltimore Album Beauty 68
Baltimore Album Nouveau With Angels 126
Beginnings, The 8
Birds A-humming, Iris A-blooming 40, 86
Blueprints 14
Carnation Carrousel 72
Cataclysm 168
Celtic Splendor 42
Color Rhythms 114
Continuum 160
Corn Crib 80
Cosmos 144
Dawn Splendor 94
Desert Blooms 112
Desert Sunrise: Desert Bontanical Gardens,
    Phoenix, AZ 82
Ebb & Flow II 78
Elizabethan Woods 146
Family Album 132
Fanciful Garden 58
Flywheels 22
Fuego En La Noche 32
Garden, The 174
Generations 172
Genetic Engineering Brings You Designer
    Christmas Trees 156
Hawaii 52
High Tech Tucks #17 76
Ice Fantasia 56
In A Galaxy Far, Far, Far, Far, Far Away 158
In The Bleak Midwinter 150
Iris Germanica 36
Jacobean Arbor 60
July 122
Kaleidoscope Stars 12
Labyrinth 34

Lilies Of The Field 108
Looking Back II: Silent Cries 90
Love Song 54
Magic Flute, The 44
Marys' Garden 124
Midwinter Night's Dream, A 10
Molly's Star 16
Nihon No Onna No Ko 100
Oh, My Stars 18
Ohio Bride's Quilt 48, 88
Ozark Oaks 98
Paradise Lost 166
Paramount Stars 62
Peace Lily 116
Peaceable Kingdom 134
Peacocks 128
Pre-pubescent Pool Party 130
R.E.M. (Rapid Eye Movement) 140
Rail Through The Rockies 104
Red Window, The 154
Reflections 74, 102
Rhapsody In Threads 24
Satin Pinwheels 28
Schools Of Modern Art 138
Shalimar Garden 38
Six x Six Comes Up Roses 142
Soul of Medieval Italy, The 84
Spinoff 120
Spring's Promise 118
Squares And Bars 162
Starburst 106
Sticks And Twigs 148
Tennessee Pink Marble 96
To England With Love 170, 176
Tokay Bouquet 26
Tulips Aglow: 1830's Revisited 66
Warning: Some Colors May Run 164
Westward Ho! 46
When Grandmother's Lily Garden Blooms 30
With Help From My Friends 50
Wyoming 64

❧American Quilter's Society❧
dedicated to publishing books for today's quilters

The following AQS publications are currently available:

- **Adapting Architectural Details for Quilts,** Carol Wagner, #2282: AQS, 1991, 88 pages, softbound, $12.95
- **American Beauties: Rose & Tulip Quilts,** Gwen Marston & Joe Cunningham, #1907: AQS, 1988, 96 pages, softbound, $14.95
- **America's Pictorial Quilts,** Caron L. Mosey, #1662: AQS, 1985, 112 pages, hardbound, $19.95
- **Applique Designs: My Mother Taught Me to Sew,** Faye Anderson, #2121: AQS, 1990, 80 pages, softbound, $12.95
- **Arkansas Quilts: Arkansas Warmth,** Arkansas Quilter's Guild, Inc., #1908: AQS, 1987, 144 pages, hardbound, $24.95
- **The Art of Hand Applique,** Laura Lee Fritz, #2122: AQS, 1990, 80 pages, softbound, $14.95
- **...Ask Helen More About Quilting Designs,** Helen Squire, #2099: AQS, 1990, 54 pages, 17 x 11, spiral-bound, $14.95
- **Award-Winning Quilts & Their Makers: Vol. I, The Best of AQS Shows – 1985-1987,** #2207: AQS, 1991, 232 pages, softbound, $24.95
- **Award-Winning Quilts & Their Makers: Vol. II, The Best of AQS Shows – 1988-1989,** #2354: AQS, 1992, 176 pages, softbound, $24.95
- **Classic Basket Quilts,** Elizabeth Porter & Marianne Fons, #2208: AQS, 1991, 128 pages, softbound, $16.95
- **A Collection of Favorite Quilts,** Judy Florence, #2119: AQS, 1990, 136 pages, softbound, $18.95
- **Creative Machine Art,** Sharee Dawn Roberts, #2355: AQS, 1992, 142 pages, 9 x 9, softbound, $24.95
- **Dear Helen, Can You Tell Me?...all about quilting designs,** Helen Squire, #1820: AQS, 1987, 51 pages, 17 x 11, spiral-bound, $12.95
- **Dye Painting!,** Ann Johnston, #3399: AQS, 1992, 88 pages, softbound, $19.95
- **Dyeing & Overdyeing of Cotton Fabrics,** Judy Mercer Tescher, #2030: AQS, 1990, 54 pages, softbound, $9.95
- **Flavor Quilts for Kids to Make: Complete Instructions for Teaching Children to Dye, Decorate & Sew Quilts,** Jennifer Amor #2356: AQS, 1991, 120 pages, softbound, $12.95
- **From Basics to Binding: A Complete Guide to Making Quilts,** Karen Kay Buckley, #2381: AQS, 1992, 160 pages, softbound, $16.95
- **Fun & Fancy Machine Quiltmaking,** Lois Smith, #1982: AQS, 1989, 144 pages, softbound, $19.95
- **Gallery of American Quilts: 1849-1988,** #1938: AQS, 1988, 128 pages, softbound, $19.95
- **Gallery of American Quilts 1860-1989: Book II,** #2129: AQS, 1990, 128 pages, softbound, $19.95
- **Gallery of American Quilts 1830-1991: Book III,** #3421: AQS, 1992, 128 pages, softbound, $19.95
- **The Grand Finale: A Quilter's Guide to Finishing Projects,** Linda Denner, #1924: AQS, 1988, 96 pages, softbound, $14.95
- **Heirloom Miniatures,** Tina M. Gravatt, #2097: AQS, 1990, 64 pages, softbound, $9.95
- **Home Study Course in Quiltmaking,** Jeannie M. Spears, #2031: AQS, 1990, 240 pages, softbound, $19.95
- **Infinite Stars,** Gayle Bong, #2283: AQS, 1992, 72 pages, softbound, $12.95
- **The Ins and Outs: Perfecting the Quilting Stitch,** Patricia J. Morris, #2120: AQS, 1990, 96 pages, softbound, $9.95
- **Irish Chain Quilts: A Workbook of Irish Chains & Related Patterns,** Joyce B. Peaden, #1906: AQS, 1988, 96 pages, softbound, $14.95
- **The Log Cabin Returns to Kentucky: Quilts from the Pilgrim/Roy Collection,** Gerald Roy and Paul Pilgrim, #3329: AQS, 1992, 36 pages, 9 x 7, softbound, $12.95
- **Marbling Fabrics for Quilts: A Guide for Learning & Teaching,** Kathy Fawcett & Carol Shoaf, #2206: AQS, 1991, 72 pages, softbound, $12.95
- **More Projects and Patterns: A Second Collection of Favorite Quilts,** Judy Florence, #3330: AQS, 1992, 152 pages, softbound, $18.95
- **Nancy Crow: Quilts and Influences,** Nancy Crow, #1981: AQS, 1990, 256 pages, 9 x 12, hardcover, $29.95
- **Nancy Crow: Work in Transition,** Nancy Crow, #3331: AQS, 1992, 32 pages, 9 x 10, softbound, $12.95
- **New Jersey Quilts – 1777 to 1950: Contributions to an American Tradition,** The Heritage Quilt Project of New Jersey; text by Rachel Cochran, Rita Erickson, Natalie Hart & Barbara Schaffer, #3332: AQS, 1992, 256 pages, softbound, $29.95
- **No Dragons on My Quilt,** Jean Ray Laury with Ritva Laury & Lizabeth Laury, #2153: AQS, 1990, 52 pages, hardcover, $12.95
- **Oklahoma Heritage Quilts,** Oklahoma Quilt Heritage Project #2032: AQS, 1990, 144 pages, softbound, $19.95
- **Quilt Groups Today: Who They Are, Where They Meet, What They Do, and How to Contact Them; A Complete Guide for 1992-1993,** #3308: AQS, 1992, 336 pages, softbound, $14.95
- **Quiltmaker's Guide: Basics & Beyond,** Carol Doak, #2284: AQS, 1992, 208 pages, softbound, $19.95
- **Quilts: The Permanent Collection – MAQS,** #2257: AQS, 1991, 100 pages, 10 x 6½, softbound, $9.95
- **Scarlet Ribbons: American Indian Technique for Today's Quilters,** Helen Kelley, #1819: AQS, 1987, 104 pages, softbound, $15.95
- **Sensational Scrap Quilts,** Darra Duffy Williamson, #2357: AQS, 1992, 152 pages, softbound, $24.95
- **Sets & Borders,** Gwen Marston & Joe Cunningham, #1821: AQS, 1987, 104 pages, softbound, $14.95
- **Somewhere in Between: Quilts and Quilters of Illinois,** Rita Barrow Barber, #1790: AQS, 1986, 78 pages, softbound, $14.95
- **Stenciled Quilts for Christmas,** Marie Monteith Sturmer, #2098: AQS, 1990, 104 pages, softbound, $14.95
- **A Treasury of Quilting Designs,** Linda Goodmon Emery, #2029: AQS, 1990, 80 pages, 14 x 11, spiral-bound, $14.95

 These books can be found in local bookstores and quilt shops. If you are unable to locate a title in your area, you can order by mail from AQS, P.O. Box 3290, Paducah, KY 42002-3290. Please add $1 for the first book and 40¢ for each additional one to cover postage and handling. (International orders please add $1.50 for the first book and $1 for each additional one.)